THE NOUVEAU ENTREPRENEUR

A Step-by-Step Guide to Start and Successfully Run a New Business

GEORGE DEVEAU

Disciaimer

The information provided in this book is for informational purposes only and is not intended to be a source of advice or credit analysis with respect to the material presented. The information and/or documents contained in this book do not constitute legal or financial advice and should never be used without first consulting with a financial professional to determine what may be best for your individual needs.

The publisher and the author do not make any guarantee or other promise as to any results that may be obtained from using the content of this book. You should never make any investment decision without first consulting with your own financial advisor and conducting your own research and due diligence. To the maximum extent permitted by law, the publisher and the author disclaim any and all liability in the event any information, commentary, analysis, opinions, advice and/or recommendations contained in this book prove to be inaccurate, incomplete or unreliable, or result in any investment or other losses.

Content contained or made available through this book is not intended to and does not constitute legal advice or investment advice and no attorney-client relationship is formed. The publisher and the author are providing this book and its contents on an "as is" basis. Your use of the information in this book is at your own risk.

Contents

Introduction

Stepping into the entrepreneurial arena is more than a career choice—it's a leap into a world of opportunity and challenge that can profoundly transform your life and community. For many, this path offers a gateway to personal growth, financial independence, and a chance to make a meaningful impact. However, the journey from concept to successful enterprise can seem daunting, especially for those without a formal business education.

My name is George Deveau, and I've walked the path on which you are about to embark. With roots in South Louisiana, education from Louisiana State University, and an MBA from Tulane University, I've navigated the path from idea to successful business launch—not just once, but four times over. My ventures have varied widely, and one proudly stood out as the #3 new company making the greatest impact in the Houston area according to the Houston Business Journal. Beyond my academic and entrepreneurial achievements, I've devoted my career to coaching and consulting, helping others realize their business potential.

'The Nouveau Entrepreneur: A Step-by-Step Guide to Start a New Enterprise' is not just another business book. It's a practical companion crafted for you—the aspiring entrepreneur, the seasoned business person, and the career shifter eager to pivot into a new venture. This guide breaks down the complexities of business, offering you a clear, practical roadmap filled with actionable advice. It's designed to show you not just the theories but the practical steps necessary to bring your business vision to life.

This guide is unique because it blends solid academic principles with the gritty realities of entrepreneurial life. You won't find just high-level theories here; instead, you'll get a toolkit filled with real-world experiences, successes, and even the missteps that provide valuable lessons. From setting up your legal framework to mastering marketing and securing financing to scaling your operation, every chapter is structured to guide you through each critical phase of building your business.

As you journey through this book, you'll be immersed in inspiring stories from those who have walked this path before you. You'll learn not only from their successes but also from the challenges they faced. These narratives are complemented by interactive elements like exercises and checklists that enhance your understanding and empower you to apply what you learn directly to your entrepreneurial endeavors. This isn't just a book-it's a tool that invites you to actively participate in your own entrepreneurial journey.

Embarking on this journey can be intimidating. Doubts and fears are common, but they shouldn't hold you back. This book addresses these concerns head-on, equipping you with the knowledge and confidence to overcome them. Think of this as your entrepreneurial toolkit, each page crafted to move you closer to turning your business idea into reality.

Let this book be your first step toward a successful entrepreneurial journey. Engage with it, challenge yourself with its exercises, and use it as a springboard to launch your enterprise with confidence and clarity. The path ahead is exciting, and I am here to guide you through each step. As your guide, I'll share my experiences, provide practical advice, and answer your questions along the way. Let's get started!

ONE

Laying the Foundations

Have you ever wondered what separates a garage band from a Grammy winner? Sometimes it's not just raw talent but the framework they build around their music—the label, the management, and even the band's legal structure. Similarly, your business's foundation is pivotal in determining its growth and success. This chapter is about correctly laying down those foundational blocks, starting with the crucial decision to select the proper business structure. Whether you're flying solo or planning to build the next big tech empire, understanding the nuances of business entities is your first step. Let's dive into the nitty-gritty of business structures, their implications, and how to choose the best one for your budding enterprise.

1.1 Choosing the Right Business Structure: From Sole Proprietorship to Corporation

Differentiate Business Entities

Choosing a business structure is like picking out a new car. You need something that suits your style, meets your needs, and fits your budget. The four main types of business entities—sole proprietorship, partnership, Limited Liability Company (LLC), and corporation—each have their own set of rules, benefits, and drawbacks.

Lets take a look at these four main types of business structures including the two main types of corporation structures.

Business structure	Ownership	Liability	Taxes
Sole proprietorship	One person	Unlimited personal liability	Self-employment tax Personal tax
Partnerships	Two or more people	Unlimited personal liability unless structured as a limited partnership	Self-employment tax (except for limited partners) Personal tax
Limited liability company (LLC)	One or more people	Owners are not personally liable	Self-employment tax Personal tax or corporate tax
Corporation - C corp	One or more people	Owners are not personally liable	Corporate tax
Corporation - S corp	One or more people, but no more than 100, and all must be U.S. citizens	Owners are not personally liable	Personal tax

Source: SBA.gov

Sole Proprietorship: Think of this as a bicycle. It's simple, inexpensive, and great for someone without much baggage. You have complete control, but with that comes the responsibility for all debts and legal actions your business might face.

A Sole Proprietorship is the most basic form of a business. You own the company yourself and are responsible for all aspects of the business. The business and the owner are one without distinction. The profits are yours, as are any losses. You are responsible for any debt incurred and all liabilities.

Partnership: This is more like a tandem bike. Two or more people share the ride, the efforts, and the risks. Partnerships are easy to form and offer more resources and ideas, but like the sole proprietorship, you and your partner(s) bear full liability.

This is the simplest structure for a business with more than one owner. Each partner shares in the profits, losses, expenses, etc. There are two types of partnerships; a Limited Partnership (LP) and a Limited Liability Partnership (LLP). A Limited Partnership has one general partner or manager who is responsible for the operations of the company, and carries unlimited liability. All of the other partners have limited liability, but also have limited control over the company's operations. A Limited Liability Partnership limits each of the owners' liabilities and protects them from debts that the company has taken. They are also protected from the actions of any of the other partners.

Limited Liability Company (LLC): Consider the LLC as your SUV. It's versatile, protecting your personal assets from business liabilities while providing operational flexibility. It's perfect for those who want protection plus simplicity.

An LLC incorporates the advantages of both corporations and partnerships. The LLC gives liability protection of a corporation and the tax benefits of a partnership.

Corporation: This is the bus. It's sturdy, can carry a number of passengers, and is designed to help you reach bigger goals. Corporations offer the strongest protection against personal liability but are costly and complex to set up and maintain. There are two main types of corporations; "C" Corporations and "S" Corporations, each with its own set of advantages.

Corporations are legal entities that issue stock and have shareholders. They provide the strongest legal and liability protections for their owners. However, they have higher setup costs and specific requirements for record-keeping, meetings, etc.

A "C" Corporation is a separate entity from the owners (shareholders). It pays its own taxes including corporate income taxes.

An "S" Corporation is similar to a "C" Corporation, but is set up to gain some tax advantages over the "C" Corporation, such as avoiding double taxation issues. There are other tax advantages such as "S" Corporation Distributions that can avoid paying some of the FICA (payroll) taxes.

Choosing the right vehicle from the start can set you on the path to success without unnecessary detours. Consultation with a knowledgable tax advisor versed in business taxes is strongly advisable here, as it may be difficult to make changes once in operation.

Tax Implications

Each business structure affects your pocketbook in different ways, especially regarding taxes. Sole proprietors pay taxes on business profits through their personal tax returns – straightforward but potentially hefty if you're making a good profit. Partnerships also pass profits and losses to your personal taxes, but you only pay on your share of the partnership.

LLCs offer flexibility. You can choose whether the IRS treats you as a sole proprietor, partnership, or corporation. The corporate tax structure could be beneficial, as corporations are taxed separately from the owners, potentially lowering your personal tax rate.

Understanding these implications helps ensure you avoid unexpected tax bills or miss out on benefits. It's crucial to consult with a tax advisor to choose the most tax-efficient structure for your specific situation.

Liability and Risk

How much risk are you comfortable taking with your personal assets? Sole proprietorships and LPs may expose you and your partners to personal liability if your business is sued or incurs debt. In contrast, LLCs, LLPs, and corporations shield your personal assets, separating them from the business's liabilities.

This protection is critical if your business operates in an industry prone to litigation or involves considerable debt. Without it, your personal assets – like your home, car, and savings – could be at risk if your business runs into legal troubles.

Once again, consultation with a tax advisor is strongly recommended.

Future Scaling and Investment

Think about where you want your business to be in five, ten, or even twenty years. A corporation might be your best bet if you aim for substantial growth or are planning to attract investors. It allows you to issue stocks, making it easier to raise capital. LLCs are also attractive for their operational flexibility and pass-through taxation, making them suitable for business owners who anticipate steady growth and possibly bringing in partners.

Selecting the proper business structure is about more than just addressing your current needs. It is also about paving the way for future opportunities and expansions. As your business evolves, so too can your structure, adapting to new challenges and scales.

1.2 Navigating Business Registration: A Step-by-Step State Guide

Registering your business is like setting up base camp before a major climb—it's the starting point of your ascent to entrepreneurial success. Each state in the U.S. has its own set of rules and requirements, which can feel like navigating a maze if you're not prepared. Whether you're in sunny California or bustling New York, understanding the specific requirements of your state is the first step to ensuring your business is built on solid ground. Let's walk through the essentials of business registration, breaking down what you'll need, where to go, and how to handle the paperwork without breaking a sweat.

State-Specific Requirements

Imagine you're planning a road trip across the country. Each state you visit might have different speed limits and road rules. Similarly, each state has distinct requirements for business registration. For instance, some states require a business to file for a state-specific tax identification number, while others use the federal EIN (Employment Identification Number) for all reporting. States like Nevada offer privacy benefits and don't require business owners to be publicly listed, whereas states like California require extensive disclosure and higher fees. To start, you'll need a checklist tailored to your state:

1. Business Name: Ensure your business name is available and meets state requirements. Do a search on your Secretary of State's website.
2. Business Structure: Confirm that the type of legal structure you've chosen (as discussed in previous sections) aligns with state requirements.
3. Registered Agent: Many states require you to have a registered agent—a person or company that will receive legal and tax documents on behalf of your business.
4. Location: Some states have zoning laws that affect where certain types of businesses can operate.
5. Licenses and Permits: Depending on your business type and location, you may need specific licenses and permits to operate legally in your state.

The Secretary of State's website for your state is a treasure trove of information, providing details on everything from forms to fees. Bookmark this site, as it will be a valuable resource throughout the life of your business. Many states offer a business startup portal where you can do name searches, business filings, tax registrations, license requirements, and other resources all in one location.

For an online link to each state, go to: https://www.e-secretaryofstate.com

Obtaining an Employee Identification Number (EIN)

The first step in setting up a new company is to obtain an Employee Identification Number from the IRS. This can be done either by mail or directly online. There is no cost to obtaining an EIN. Unless you are a Sole Proprietor you will need to obtain an EIN, and there are certain situations where even a Sole Proprietor will need an EIN. Typically an EIN can be obtained within 24 hours by filing with the IRS online.

To obtain an EIN online go to: https://www.irs.gov/businesses/ small-businesses-self-employed/apply-for-an-employer-identifica tion-number-ein-online

Registration Process

The actual process of registering your business can feel as daunting as doing your taxes for the first time. However, with the proper preparation, it can be as straightforward as filling out a few forms. Generally, you'll start by filing your "Articles of Incorporation" (for corporations), "Articles of Organization" (for LLCs), or "Certificates of Formation" for partnerships with the state's business filing agency, the Secretary of State. This document includes basic information about your business, such as your business name, purpose, and the details of your registered agent.

You can often file these documents online, which speeds up the process and ensures you're not stuck waiting in line or dealing with mail delays. After filing, you'll receive a confirmation that your business is officially registered. That moment, receiving confirmation, feels like seeing your business name on a door for the first time—it's tangible proof that your business officially exists.

Costs Involved

Starting a business comes with its costs, much like any significant endeavor. When budgeting for business registration, consider the following:

1. Filing Fees: These vary from state to state. For example, filing Articles of Organization for an LLC in Arizona might cost around $50, while in Massachusetts, the fee can be as high as $500.
2. Registered Agent Fees: If you decide to use a professional registered agent service, these can range from $100 to $300 per year.
3. Professional Fees: Hiring an attorney or accountant to help with your registration can ensure accuracy and compliance, but it will also increase your startup costs.
4. Licenses and Permits: Depending on your business type and location, you might also need to budget for various licenses and permits.

While these costs can add up, consider them an investment in the stability and legality of your business. It's like buying quality gear for a trek—you want to ensure you're well-equipped to avoid any pitfalls along the way.

Renewals and Compliance

Once your business is registered, the work isn't over. Staying compliant is like keeping your business in tune. Most states require businesses to file annual reports and renew some licenses and permits. These filings ensure that your business information is up-to-date and that you're operating in accordance with state laws. Failure to comply with these requirements can lead to fines, notices, and sometimes the dissolution of your business.

Keeping a calendar of due dates for all your compliance requirements can be a lifesaver. Tools like Google Calendar or business management software can send you reminders as deadlines approach, ensuring you never miss a filing. Remember, staying compliant not only keeps you out of trouble but also builds your business's credibility and trustworthiness.

1.3 Understanding Business Licenses and Permits: What You Need and How to Get Them

Navigating the maze of business licenses and permits is like trying to solve a complex puzzle. Each piece represents a specific legal requirement that your business must comply with to operate smoothly and legally. Whether you're setting up a cozy café in the heart of the city or launching a tech startup, understanding which licenses and permits you need, how to apply for them, and who oversees these requirements is crucial. This isn't just about ticking boxes; it's about laying a compliant foundation for your business that safeguards you from potential legal complications.

Identify Necessary Licenses and Permits

The first step is determining which licenses and permits your business requires, which can vary dramatically depending on your business activities, location, and industry regulations. For instance, if you're opening a restaurant, you'll need health permits, building permits, signage permits, and possibly a liquor license, each governed by different authorities. On the other hand, a freelance graphic designer may only need a basic business operation license.

Start with your local city or county government office to determine your needs. Often, they provide a checklist of required licenses and permits for various types of businesses. Additionally, you can consult industry-specific associations, which offer resources and guidance tailored to particular business sectors.

Visit the U.S. Small Business Administration (SBA) website for practical steps. The SBA website offers a tool that lists federal, state, and local permits, licenses, and registrations you'll need to run a business. By entering your zip code and business type, you can quickly see a tailored list of what you need to obtain. Remember, handling this in the early stages of setting up your business prevents operational hiccups down the road, making it a critical step in your setup process.

See https://www.sba.gov

Application Process

Once you know what you need, the next step is the application process, which can be daunting given the bureaucratic hurdles often involved. Each license or permit will have its own application process, fees, and timeline. Start by gathering all necessary documentation, which can include your business plan, incorporation documents, and proof of identity and address. It's similar to assembling all the essential ingredients before you begin cooking a complex dish.

Many local government websites now allow you to apply for licenses and permits online, which can save you a significant amount of time. However, you might need to visit in person to provide documents or attend an interview for some permits. Patience is key here. Local government offices are often overloaded, and it can take time to process your application. Keep copies of all submissions and a record of all communications. In some cases, hiring a professional, like a lawyer or a permit service, might be worth the cost to navigate this complex process efficiently, especially if your business requires multiple or complicated licenses.

Regulatory Bodies

Understanding which regulatory bodies oversee your business licensing and permits can provide you with direct access to authoritative information and support. For example, the Environmental Protection Agency (EPA) oversees businesses that could impact the environment, requiring specific permits regarding air emissions or waste management. Similarly, the Department of Health would be your go-to for any business related to food services, healthcare, or anything that impacts public health.

For most startups, the local city or county clerk's office is a primary contact point for business licenses. It's also advisable to connect with state and federal agencies relevant to your specific business. For instance, if you're starting a business that involves broadcasting or telecommunications, you'll need to check in with the Federal Communications Commission (FCC). Each agency usually has a help desk or a resource center for businesses to get more information and assistance.

Maintaining Compliance

Staying compliant is an ongoing process. Business licenses and permits are not 'set and forget' items. Many require annual renewals, and failing to update them can lead to fines, penalties, or even the closure of your business. Set up a compliance calendar to track renewal dates, reporting deadlines, and other compliance-related events. Tools like Google Calendar or specialized compliance software can help you stay on top of these dates without having to manually track each requirement.

Moreover, staying informed about changes in legislation that may affect your business is crucial. Regulatory environments are not static, and new laws can introduce new licensing requirements or modify existing ones. Regularly reviewing your local government and industry-specific news will keep you informed of any changes that might affect your business, allowing you to anticipate and adapt to changes without scrambling at the last minute.

In essence, understanding and managing your business licenses and permits ensures that your business operates within the legal frameworks established by various authorities. By taking a proactive approach to this task, you not only protect yourself from legal issues but also establish your credibility as a reliable and trustworthy business operator. This diligence pays off by paving the way for smooth operations and sustainable growth, letting you focus more on what you do best—running your business.

1.4 The Essentials of Intellectual Property: Protecting Your Ideas

Intellectual property (IP) is the secret sauce to your business recipe—it sets you apart in a crowded marketplace and can be your ticket to sustainable success. In today's hyper-competitive business environment, protecting your intellectual creations is not just a legal necessity; it's a strategic asset. Whether it's the unique design of your product, a breakthrough software, or the distinctive name of your company, understanding the different types of IP and how to protect them is crucial for any entrepreneur.

Types of Intellectual Property: Let's break down the main types of IP you might encounter in your business journey. First up, we have **patents**, which are all about inventions. These can be products or processes that offer a new way of doing something or provide a new technical solution. For example, if you invent a new type of eco-friendly packaging material, a patent might protect your invention from being made, used, or sold by others without your permission.

Next are **trademarks**, which protect symbols, names, and slogans used to distinguish your goods or services. Think of the iconic Nike swoosh or the catchy phrase "Just Do It." These trademarks are instantly recognizable and differentiate Nike's products in the marketplace.

Then, we have **copyrights**, which cover literary and artistic works like books, music, movies, business materials such as software code, and even marketing content. If you create a unique software program for financial management, copyright law prevents others from copying or redistributing your software without your consent.

Lastly, there's something called **trade secrets**, which include formulas, practices, or designs that are confidential and provide a business advantage over competitors. A classic example is the secret blend of 11 herbs and spices used in KFC's fried chicken.

Protection Strategies: Now, knowing what types of IP exist isn't enough; you need to know how to protect them. Registering your IP is often the first and most crucial step. For patents, this means filing an application with the patent office and providing a detailed description of your invention. For trademarks, you need to register them at the national or international level, depending on where you plan to do business. Copyright protection, on the other hand, is automatic from the moment you create a work, but registering it can provide additional legal benefits like statutory damages in case of infringement.

Monitoring your IP is just as important as registering it. Use online tools and services to keep an eye on how your IP is being used or misused online. Setting up Google Alerts for your trademarks or regularly checking patent databases can help you spot infringements before they cause significant damage.

Avoiding Infringement: While protecting your IP, you also need to ensure you're not stepping on anyone else's toes. Conducting thorough IP searches before launching a new product or service is essential. This means checking patent databases to ensure your new invention doesn't infringe on existing patents, searching trademark registers to confirm your brand name or logo isn't too similar to existing ones, and ensuring any content you use is either original or appropriately licensed.

Leveraging IP for Business Advantage: Effectively managed IP does more than just protect your assets—it can also be a significant business advantage. IP can enhance your valuation in the eyes of investors and partners, serve as collateral for loans, and even provide a steady revenue stream through licensing deals. For instance, if you hold a patent, you can license it to other companies for a fee, creating a new revenue stream without the need to directly market or sell the product yourself.

Moreover, a strong IP portfolio can act as a deterrent to competitors, preventing them from entering your market space or copying your innovations. In some industries, like technology or pharmaceuticals, a robust IP portfolio can be the deciding factor in a company's ability to compete and survive.

Understanding and managing intellectual property is not just about legal protection; it's about setting up your business for growth, innovation, and long-term success. By effectively securing and leveraging your intellectual assets, you ensure that your business not only survives but thrives in the competitive global marketplace.

1.5 Business Insurance Demystified: What You Need to Safeguard Your Enterprise

Navigating the world of business insurance can sometimes feel like trying to comprehend a foreign language menu without a translator. You know you need something substantial to sustain your business, but making the right choices can often seem daunting. Let's simplify this. Think of business insurance as a safety net —it's there to catch you in case things go wrong, and in business, a number of things can go awry. From liability issues to property damage, having the proper insurance policies in place can be the difference between a minor setback and a major catastrophe.

Types of Business Insurance

First, let's unpack the different types of insurance you might consider. **Liability insurance** is like wearing a seatbelt; it protects you in case someone gets hurt as a result of your business activities. If a customer slips and falls at your store or your product causes harm, liability insurance helps cover the legal fees and any settlements that may result.

Property insurance, on the other hand, is like a sturdy helmet for your business assets. It covers the physical assets of your business —like your equipment, inventory, and office space—against damage from fires, storms, or burglaries.

Then there's **worker's compensation insurance**, which is mandatory in most states if you have employees. This type of insurance acts like a financial airbag, providing wage replacement and medical benefits to employees injured in the course of employment. In return for these benefits, employees give up their rights to sue their employer for the incident.

Lastly, **professional liability insurance**, or errors and omissions insurance (E&O), is crucial if your business provides services or advice. It's like an error-correcting code in a software program, offering protection against claims of negligence or harm due to mistakes or failure to perform.

Assessing Needs

Determining which insurance policies are right for your business involves a clear assessment of your risks, which vary widely depending on your industry, location, and size. Start by evaluating the physical risks associated with your business environment—are you located in an area prone to natural disasters? Do your operations involve hazardous materials? Also, consider the human element—are you providing a service that could lead to professional liability claims? Understanding these factors will guide you in selecting the appropriate level of coverage.

For instance, freelance graphic designers might prioritize professional liability insurance over property insurance if they work from home with minimal equipment. In contrast, restaurant owners would need robust policies covering property, liability, and worker's compensation, given the risks associated with high foot traffic and kitchen operations.

Choosing a Provider

Selecting an insurance provider is like choosing a long-term business partner—you need reliability, trust, and a mutual understanding of your business goals. Start by comparing quotes from several providers to get a sense of the market. However, don't make your decision based solely on price. Consider the provider's reputation, the ease of filing claims, and the quality of customer service. It's also wise to check reviews and testimonials from other business owners, especially those in your industry.

It's beneficial to consult with an insurance broker who can offer impartial advice tailored to your specific needs. A broker can help you navigate the complex terms and conditions and ensure you get the best coverage for your budget. Remember, your insurance needs will evolve as your business grows, so choose a provider that can scale with you.

Policy Management

Just as you regularly tune up your vehicle to keep it running smoothly, you should also periodically review and update your insurance policies. As your business grows, you might purchase new equipment, hire more employees, or expand your services, all of which could alter your insurance needs. An annual review of your policies helps ensure you're adequately covered and not over-paying for unnecessary coverage.

Managing your business insurance effectively means staying proactive, not just when you first purchase your policies but as an ongoing strategy to protect your enterprise.

Regular reviews, a clear understanding of your needs, and a reliable provider set the foundation for a secure business environment, allowing you to focus on growth and innovation.

1.6 Setting Up Your Business Bank Account and Accounting Basics

Navigating the financial aspects of your new business can sometimes feel like you're learning to drive a stick shift in a hilly city. It's tricky, but it becomes second nature once you get the hang of it. This starts with setting up your business bank account, which not only simplifies your financial management but also adds a layer of professionalism and credibility to your operations. Let's break down how to choose the right bank and account type, open your business account, and understand the basic accounting principles that will keep you on track.

Choosing the Right Bank and Account Type

Think of choosing a bank with the understanding that it will be a base for your operations. You want a secure, accessible, and resourceful home for your finances. Different banks offer various benefits; some may offer excellent customer service and low fees, while others may provide powerful online tools or better interest rates. The key is to find the right fit for your business needs.

Business banking accounts generally come in a few flavors: checking accounts, savings accounts, merchant services accounts, and credit accounts. A *business checking account* is essential for managing day-to-day transactions, paying bills, and handling payroll. Think of it as your day-to-day operational hub. *Savings accounts*, meanwhile, are your long-term reserves, ideal for stashing profits and earning interest over time.

Merchant services accounts are crucial if you accept credit card transactions, as they provide a way to process these payments smoothly. Lastly, *credit accounts* can help manage cash flow with credit cards or lines of credit, offering a cushion when cash is tight or enabling you to make significant purchases without dipping into your savings.

When selecting a bank, consider how each account type fits with your business model. A retail store might need robust merchant services, while a freelance consultant might prioritize a good credit account for occasional travel expenses. Also, weigh the fees, minimum balance requirements, and interest rates. Sometimes, the bank with a slightly higher fee provides superior services and tech support that could save you money in the long run.

Opening a Business Account

Opening your business bank account is a significant milestone. It's one of those moments in your business setup that makes things feel 'real.' But it's not just about walking into a bank and opening an account; there are a few steps and considerations to ensure everything goes smoothly.

First, you'll need your business documentation in order. Depending on your business structure, this might include your EIN (Employer Identification Number), incorporation documents, and ownership agreements. Each bank may require different documents, so it's a good practice to call ahead or check online for a specific list.

Once you have your documents, the next step is opening the account. This can often be completed online, but doing it in person can provide a valuable opportunity to establish a relationship with the bank. Ask questions, understand precisely what you're signing up for, and make sure you're aware of all the fees and regulations associated with your new account.

Beware of common pitfalls during this process. For instance, mixing personal and business banking might seem more manageable in the early days, but it can create significant headaches and legal issues down the line. **From the start, ensuring your business finances are separate from your personal accounts establishes financial discipline and simplifies accounting processes.**

Basic Accounting Principles

Whether you love them or dread them, basic accounting principles are crucial for keeping your business on solid financial footing. Understanding these principles can help you make informed decisions, manage your cash flow effectively, and prepare for future growth.

Even if you hire an accountant or a bookkeeper you need to understand the basic principles of how to handle your business finances to effectively manage your cash flow. Several courses are available to do so. One of the more popular is by QuickBooks; here is the link: https://quickbooks.intuit.com/r/bookkeeping/bookkeeping-courses-online/

One fundamental concept is *double-entry bookkeeping*. For every transaction, two entries are made: one to a debit account and one to a credit account. This method provides a complete view of your financial activities and helps keep your books balanced, ensuring every dollar is accounted for.

Another critical skill is reading and understanding financial statements. The three main types you'll encounter are the *balance sheet*, *income statement*, and *cash flow statement*. The balance sheet provides a snapshot of your business's financial standing at a specific point in time, showing what you own (assets) versus what you owe (liabilities and equity). The income statement, or profit and loss statement (known as the P&L), shows how much money you made and spent over a period of time. It's crucial for tracking profitability. Lastly, the cash flow statement breaks down the actual cash coming in and going out, helping you manage your liquidity.

There are two methods by which accounting systems are set up and run: cash accounting and accrual accounting. Basic businesses may be able to operate on a cash basis, where they log all transactions when they make or receive payments. Most companies, however, will operate on an accrual basis. An accrual accounting system will allow you to categorize income and expenses in the period when they originate, even though the payments or receipts may occur in a different accounting period. Businesses that plan or expect growth should prepare for the future, which will generally require accrual accounting.

See your CPA or tax professional for more information.

Financial Software and Tools

Modern software and tools can be a lifesaver for those not versed in the intricacies of financial management, automating many of the processes that once required an accountant. Tools like QuickBooks, FreshBooks, and Xero offer user-friendly interfaces that handle everything from invoicing and payroll to tax preparation and expense tracking. They can connect directly to your bank accounts and credit cards, streamlining data entry and reducing errors.

Choosing the right tools depends on your specific needs— consider factors like the size of your business, the complexity of your financial transactions, and your budget. Many of these tools offer scalable solutions that grow with your business, adding features and capabilities as your financial management needs become more complex.

Setting up your business bank account and understanding basic accounting principles are not just administrative tasks; they are fundamental to your business's healthy operation and growth. By taking the time to set up the right financial structures and understand the basics of keeping your books, you're building a framework that supports not just your business's current transactions but also its long-term financial health.

TWO

Financing Your Venture

P icture this: you're back in your high school days, stepping up to the plate in a crucial baseball game, bat in hand, eyes fixed on the pitcher. The crowd is buzzing, your palms are sweaty, but you're ready. This is your moment. Now, fast forward to the present—this time, the baseball diamond is the business world, and instead of a bat, you've got your business plan. The pitcher? Potential investors. It's just as thrilling, and yes, the stakes are just as high. Securing funding is one of the most exhilarating parts of your entrepreneurial adventure, and it begins with mastering the art of the pitch. Here's how to knock it out of the park.

2.1 Crafting a Winning Pitch to Investors: A Template for Success

Structuring Your Pitch--The Business Plan

Creating a compelling investor pitch is akin to writing a hit song—it needs strong opening, a catchy rhythm, and an unforgettable finale. Start with your **business model**: clearly define what your business does, who your customers are, and how you make money. Simplicity is key here; think of it as your elevator pitch—if you can't explain your business clearly in a minute, it's back to the drawing board.

Next, dive into the **market analysis**. Here, you're painting a picture of the landscape you're entering, complete with its opportunities and threats. Show investors you've done your homework by detailing market size, growth potential, and your target demographic. Use data to back your claims—investors need to see numbers, not just passion.

Then, hit them with your **financial projections**. This is your chance to show you're not just a dreamer but a savvy businessperson. Outline your expected revenue, profit margins, and cash flow over the next three to five years. Be realistic—over-optimistic forecasts can undermine your credibility.

Finally, wrap up with why your business is a unique opportunity. What sets you apart from the competition? Whether it's a revolutionary product, a patent, or an untapped market, ensure this is a highlight of your presentation.

Understanding Investor Mindset

Investors are like seasoned coaches scouting for the top athletes; they're looking for potential, but they're also assessing risk. They typically gravitate towards businesses with high scalability, meaning your idea should have the potential to grow significantly without equally significant expenses. Show them how your business can scale up and what that path might look like.

Investors also want to see a return on their investment, so highlight the potential for high returns. This doesn't just mean showing profit margins; it means demonstrating a deep understanding of your business model and market, proving that you can execute your plan effectively.

Lastly, no investor wants to back a one-person show; they want a team that can weather the ups and downs of startup life. Highlight the strengths and expertise of your team members, underscoring how their experiences and skills will contribute to the success of the business.

Common Pitfalls in Pitching

Many entrepreneurs falter by either overestimating their valuation or underestimating the competition. Valuation is an art, not a science, but it needs to be grounded in reality. Overvaluing your company can scare off investors or, worse-- lead to a bad deal where you give away too much equity. As for competition, acknowledging it is not a sign of weakness. Recognize other players in the market and clearly articulate how your business is different and what gives you a competitive edge.

Another common misstep is not anticipating potential questions from investors. They might probe areas you had yet to consider important, like regulatory issues, intellectual property rights, or exit strategies. Being unprepared for these questions can make you look amateurish and unprepared.

Pitch Practice and Feedback

Like any great performance, practice is essential. Pitch in front of friends, family, or mentors—anyone who can give you construc-tive feedback. Take every piece of feedback seriously, whether it's about your delivery or the content of your pitch. Use it to refine and strengthen your presentation.

Consider recording yourself during practice sessions to critique your performance. Pay attention to not just what you say but how you say it. Are you speaking clearly and confidently? Are your slides readable and your graphs understandable? Fine-tuning these details can make a big difference in how your pitch is received.

This is precisely what the show "Shark Tank" is all about. A group of investors listen to various entrepreneurs "pitching" their product or service. If the pitch is good enough, they may obtain one or more "Shark" investors for their product or service.

Remember, your pitch isn't just a presentation; it's a performance that could determine the future of your business. By understanding your audience, perfecting your pitch structure, and embracing continuous improvement, you're setting the stage for success. So take a deep breath, step up to the plate, and swing for the fences. Your dream deserves no less.

2.2 Crowdfunding Strategies: Choosing the Right Platform and Campaign

Imagine you're setting up a lemonade stand in your neighborhood. Where you place your stand can either make you the talk of the town or just another unnoticed corner fixture. This same logic applies to selecting a crowdfunding platform—where you set up can significantly impact the success of your campaign. Crowdfunding platforms like Kickstarter, Indiegogo, and GoFundMe each have their unique audiences, fee structures, and success stories. Choosing the right one is not just about who offers the lowest fees but where your project will likely resonate most strongly.

Kickstarting your project on Kickstarter makes sense if you're aiming for a product-based business, especially in the design, technology, or arts sectors. Kickstarter's all-or-nothing model means you must reach your funding goal to receive any money, which can be a high-stakes, high-reward scenario. It's perfect if you have a flashy project that can generate a lot of buzz and attract backers looking for the next big thing. On the other hand, Indiegogo offers more flexibility with its funding models, allowing you to choose between fixed (all-or-nothing) and flexible (keep-what-you-raise) options. This platform is excellent if you need some funding no matter what and are looking to tap into a community that loves innovation across various fields, including community projects and personal finance.

GoFundMe, while typically associated with personal fundraising, has been a powerful platform for social entrepreneurship and community-based projects. If your project has a solid personal story or community focus, GoFundame might help you reach sympathetic audiences ready to support your cause. Understanding these nuances allows you to tailor your campaign strategy to the platform that best matches your project's nature and your financial needs, maximizing your chances for a successful crowdfunding campaign.

Designing a Compelling Campaign

Crafting your crowdfunding campaign is akin to telling a captivating story where you are both the author and the protagonist. The plot revolves around your project with the ultimate climax being the successful funding of your idea. Begin with setting realistic goals. Shooting for the stars is tempting, but remember, on platforms like Kickstarter, not meeting your goal could mean walking away with nothing. Research similar projects, understand what's achievable, and set a target that challenges you yet is attainable.

The rewards you offer can significantly spice up your story. These are the perks that backers will get in exchange for their pledges. Creativity wins this game; therefore, think beyond just offering the product itself. Possibly backers could get a personalized version of the product, a behind-the-scenes look into your process, or even an experience related to your project. For example, if you're launching a new coffee shop, rewards could range from a custom brew named after high-tier backers to coffee-tasting sessions for those who contribute a certain amount.

Crafting a compelling narrative is crucial. This is your chance to connect emotionally with potential backers. Share your journey, the challenges you've faced, and how your project is going to change the world—or at least your world. Videos are particularly effective in crowdfunding campaigns as they provide a dynamic way to convey your passion and professionalism. They allow you to create a richer, more personal connection with potential backers.

Marketing Your Campaign

Now that your campaign has been crafted, it's time to shout it from the rooftops. Leveraging social media platforms can amplify your voice, but each platform has its nuances. For instance, Instagram and Pinterest are great for highly visual projects thanks to their image-focused layouts, making them perfect for design or lifestyle product pitches. With its rapid-fire style, X (formerly known as Twitter) is ideal for constant, real-time updates and building buzz around countdowns or breaking news about your project.

Email marketing is another powerful tool at your disposal. It allows for more direct and personal communication. Segment your audience and tailor your messages:

- Inform potential backers about the launch.
- Update them on your progress.
- Remind them as your campaign nears its end.

Personal stories or testimonials can make these emails feel more personal and less sales-y.

Don't forget offline methods. Local events, pop-ups, or meetups can engage the community and get people talking about your project. These interactions can be powerful, turning local backers into ardent supporters who share your project with their own networks.

Post-Campaign Follow-Up

Your campaign's end is just the beginning of your journey with your backers. The follow-up can significantly impact your reputation and ability to launch future projects. Start by expressing heartfelt thanks to your backers—consider a thank you video or personalized messages. Then, keep the lines of communication open by updating them on the progress of bringing the project to life and any delays or challenges you might face. Transparency builds trust, and backers appreciate being kept in the loop.

Fulfilling your promises is non-negotiable. Deliver the rewards you committed to on time and as described. If physical products are involved, ensure they are of high quality and match the backers' expectations based on your campaign. If there are unavoidable delays, communicate these early and with clear reasons why.

Engaging your backers beyond the campaign can transform them into long-term supporters of your brand. Consider creating a community around your project, using platforms like Facebook Groups or regular newsletters to keep the conversation going.

This community can be invaluable for feedback, support, and the potential success of future projects.

2.3 Navigating Small Business Loans: A Comparison of Options

Securing a small business loan can often feel like navigating a labyrinth designed by someone who, frankly, didn't leave you a map. But fear not, because understanding the different types of loans available, their respective eligibility criteria, and the intricacies of loan agreements can transform this confusing maze into a straightforward path to securing the funding your business needs to grow and thrive.

Types of Loans Available

Let's break down the various types of small business loans you might encounter on your quest for funding. First, we have traditional bank loans, which are often the first option that comes to mind. These loans can offer competitive interest rates and extended repayment terms, but they also come with stringent eligibility criteria, including strong credit scores, solid business plans, and often, collateral. They're like the old-school diner of financing—reliable but with a high barrier to entry.

Next, there are SBA loans, which are partially guaranteed by the Small Business Administration. Think of these as your local government's endorsement of your entrepreneurial spirit. They typically offer lower down payments, flexible overhead requirements, and no collateral for some loans. However, the application process can be lengthy and complex, requiring a lot of paperwork and patience. The SBA does offer microloans for smaller amounts of capital. These loans come with a simplified application and less stringent requirements.

Then there's a whole universe of alternative lending options, including online loans, merchant cash advances, and invoice financing. These are more like your trendy food trucks, offering convenient, fast, and often innovative funding solutions that are perfect for business owners needing quick capital or not meeting the traditional bank loan criteria. For instance, online lenders might offer a speedy approval process and less stringent credit requirements, but this convenience often comes at the cost of higher interest rates.

Understanding the pros and cons of each loan type can help you select the best option based on your current needs, financial health, and business goals. It's about matching the correct type of loan to your unique situation, much like picking the right location for your new store or the best software for your daily operations.

Eligibility and Application Process

Navigating the eligibility requirements and application processes for these loans can be daunting. To increase your chances of approval, start by getting your financial ducks in a row. Ensure your business credit score is in good shape, as this is a crucial factor lenders consider. You can check your credit score through major credit bureaus or, for a more detailed insight, use services that provide a comprehensive look at your credit and financial standing.

Prepare a detailed business plan that outlines your business model, revenue streams, and growth projections. Lenders want to see that you have a clear roadmap for success and a solid understanding of your market. Additionally, gather all necessary documents beforehand, including tax returns, financial statements, legal documents like your business license, and any lease agreements.

When you apply, tailor your application to highlight the strengths of your business that align with the lender's criteria. For instance, if applying for an SBA loan, emphasize your business's potential for growth and job creation. If opting for an alternative lender, you should focus on your recent sales history and cash flow, which demonstrates your ability to repay the loan.

Understanding Terms and Conditions

Loan agreements are not the easiest reads, but understanding the terms and conditions is crucial. Key terms you'll encounter include:

- The interest rate, which dictates how much extra you'll pay back on top of the borrowed amount.
- The repayment terms, which outline how long you have to pay back the loan and how frequently payments must be made.
- Any collateral requirements, which involve assigning assets like real estate or equipment as security for the loan.

Pay close attention to the fine print regarding fees, penalties for early repayment, and what happens in case of default. Some loans have variable interest rates, which means the amount you pay can increase depending on market conditions. Others may include balloon payments, where smaller payments are made initially, followed by a large lump sum. Understanding these terms helps you avoid surprises and plan your finances accordingly.

Building a Relationship with Lenders

Finally, building a solid relationship with your lender can pay dividends. Approach this relationship as you would with a key business partner or an important customer. Be transparent about your business performance and proactive in communication. If you foresee challenges that affect your ability to make timely payments, discuss these with your lender early to explore possible adjustments to your payment schedule.

Regular updates about your business's growth, new products, or markets not only keep the lender informed but also demonstrate your commitment to the business's success. This can be invaluable should you need to renegotiate terms or seek future additional funding. Lenders are more than just financiers; they can also be partners in your business's journey, offering advice, resources, and support as you expand and evolve.

2.4 Bootstrapping Your Business: How to Minimize Costs and Maximize Resources

Bootstrapping might sound like a term fresh out of a rugged wilderness adventure, but in the business world, it's all about self-funding your startup by stretching resources as far as they can go. This approach isn't just about keeping your wallet tight; it's a strategic choice to fuel growth without sacrificing equity or control. Imagine you're starting a bakery. Instead of seeking external investors to purchase top-of-the-line equipment, you start with enough to manage initial orders and reinvest the profits to scale operations. Companies like Spanx and GoPro started this way, turning modest beginnings into blockbuster brands without initial external capital.

One of the most compelling benefits of bootstrapping is the control it allows you to maintain. Without investors or shareholders, you call the shots, making decisions quickly without needing consensus from a Board of Directors. This agility can be crucial in the early stages when you're still fine-tuning your business model. Additionally, the financial discipline required to bootstrap can lead to a lean, efficient company with a strong foundation for future growth.

There may be better strategies than going it alone for some. If you lack business financial acumen it may be beneficial to have outside interests for consultation and advice, and also to discuss the advantages and disadvantages of certain financial decisions.

To bootstrap effectively, start by embracing cost-effective strategies. Today's digital landscape is bursting with free or low-cost tools designed to streamline business operations. From open-source software for website building and graphic design to free accounting tools like Wave, these resources can save you significant amounts upfront. Another strategy is to outsource non-core tasks. Platforms like Upwork or Fiverr connect you with freelancers who can handle everything from social media marketing to bookkeeping at a fraction of the cost of hiring full-time employees.

Negotiating with suppliers is another way to cut costs. For instance, if you're opening that bakery, negotiate longer payment terms or bulk discounts with suppliers. This can free up cash flow, allowing you to invest in other areas of your business. Remember, every dollar you save is a dollar that can be reinvested into growing your business.

Resource optimization is vital when funds are limited. One approach is to reuse materials wherever possible. If launching a product, consider using recycled materials or repurposing older equipment. Not only can this reduce costs, but it also appeals to environmentally conscious consumers. Another strategy is to take advantage of business incubators. These organizations support startups by providing resources like office space, mentoring, and sometimes even funding. By reducing overhead costs you can focus more on product development and customer acquisition.

Employing just-in-time (JIT) inventory management can also streamline operations and reduce costs. This strategy aligns raw material orders from suppliers directly with production schedules, minimizing inventory costs. For example, if you manufacture smartphone cases, you order materials to arrive just as you're ready to start production, thus avoiding large amounts of unsold stock sitting in a warehouse.

Balancing growth and spending is arguably the most challenging aspect of bootstrapping. It's about knowing when to tighten the purse strings and when to open them just enough to seize growth opportunities. Reinvesting profits back into the business is a fundamental practice here. It's about making strategic choices—investing in areas that will drive revenue growth or improve operational efficiency.

For instance, after your initial success at the bakery, you may decide to purchase a larger mixer that doubles production capacity. This is a calculated decision to reinvest profits that will likely increase sales and, subsequently, profits. However, it's crucial to avoid overextending financially. Continually assess the risk versus reward of every investment, ensuring it aligns with your long-term business goals.

Occasionally, even bootstrapped businesses might need external funding to scale significantly. The key is to do this from a position of strength. If you've built a solid business foundation and kept your books green, you'll likely secure much more favorable terms from lenders or investors. This strategic approach ensures that when you seek external funds, it's on your terms and for growth, not survival.

Navigating the bootstrapping path requires a mix of creativity, discipline, and a keen eye for opportunity. It's about making the most of what you have while always keeping an eye on the horizon for the next opportunity to advance your business.

2.5 Financial Planning and Forecasting: Tools for Stability and Growth

When you're steering your business through the market's ever-changing landscape, having a solid financial plan and the ability to forecast future scenarios is like having a high-quality GPS system in your car. It not only tells you where you are but also helps you make informed decisions about which roads to take and which ones to avoid. Let's start with creating financial projections, an essential tool that can give both you and potential investors a clear picture of your company's health and trajectory.

It's like the old adage: If you don't know where you are going, then how will you know when you get there?

Creating Financial Projections

Imagine you're planning a road trip. You'll need a map, some good music, and a clear idea of where to stop for gas, food, and rest. Financial projections in business serve a similar purpose—they outline the route your company intends to take financially over the next few years. Sales forecasts, expense budgets, and cash flow statements are the main components. To begin, utilize templates or software tools like Excel or more sophisticated systems like QuickBooks or PlanGuru to help you organize and calculate these projections. Start with your sales forecast by analyzing past sales data and market conditions to predict future sales. This involves understanding seasonal trends in your industry, the impact of marketing strategies, and broader economic conditions. Next, detail your expense budget, which should include fixed costs like rent and salaries, and variable costs such as materials and marketing expenses. Being precise here helps you manage your resources efficiently. Lastly, your cash flow statement will show the actual movement of cash in and out of your business. This is crucial because it highlights the liquidity of your business, showing not just if you're profitable but if you're maintaining enough cash on hand to keep the business running smoothly.

Scenario Planning

Now, let's talk about scenario planning, which is like having different plans for your road trip depending on the weather. In business, this means preparing for various possible futures, such as a sudden market downturn or an unexpected surge in demand. This strategy involves creating "what if" scenarios to visualize how your business will handle potential challenges or opportunities. For example, what if a new competitor enters the market or a key supplier goes out of business? How will these affect your sales and expenses? Tools like financial modeling software can help you simulate these scenarios. By adjusting various parameters, you can see how changes in the market or your business operations might affect your financial health. This preparation is invaluable because it allows you to make decisions quickly and confidently when unexpected events occur.

This is where a good cash flow analysis will come into play. Changing market conditions will directly impact your cash flow, and being able to predict and address these changes ahead of time can prevent you from getting into a financial bind.

Monitoring Financial Performance

Keeping a close eye on how your business performs financially is like checking your car's dashboard. It prevents minor issues from turning into larger problems. Set up systems to regularly monitor your financial performance against the projections you've made. This is where Key Performance Indicators (KPIs) come into play. Common financial KPIs include net profit margin, gross margin, and current ratio. These indicators help you gauge the overall financial health of your business, showing you areas that are performing well and others that might need more attention.

Adjusting Business Plans

Finally, the ability to adapt is crucial. Think of it as deciding to take a scenic detour on your road trip because you've heard there's heavy traffic on your planned route. If your financial monitoring shows you're consistently missing your sales targets or your expenses are higher than projected, it may be time to adjust your business plan. This could mean pivoting your marketing strategy, cutting unnecessary costs, or possibly even changing your business model. The key is to be flexible and responsive. Regularly reviewing your business plan in light of your financial performance and the current market conditions helps you stay agile. This not only ensures you're working towards realistic and relevant goals but also prepares you to capitalize on opportunities as they arise.

Navigating the complexities of financial planning and forecasting might seem daunting at first, just like planning a big road trip. But with the right tools and a clear understanding of where you want to go, you can make it an enjoyable and highly rewarding journey that keeps your business on the path to success.

2.6 Managing Cash Flow: Techniques to Keep Your Business Solvent

Understanding the ebb and flow of your business's cash is like keeping an eye on the fuel gauge during a long road trip. Just as you would want to avoid running out of gas in the middle of nowhere, ensuring you always have enough cash on hand is critical to avoid stalling out before reaching your next milestone. Cash flow, distinct from profit, represents the actual amount of money flowing in and out of your business. Profit might show on paper, but cash flow is the money you can actually touch, and it's vital for daily operations--from paying rent to buying supplies to covering payroll.

Effective cash flow management starts with robust invoice management. Timely invoicing and follow-ups ensure that the cash keeps flowing. Consider payment terms that incentivize early payments and penalties for late payments to encourage quicker turnaround. Automating your invoicing process can save time and reduce errors, ensuring consistent cash flow.

Controlling expenditures is equally important. Regularly review your expenses to identify areas where you can cut back without compromising the quality of your products or services. This might mean renegotiating contracts with suppliers or finding more cost-effective alternatives for your operational needs. Also, consider how you can delay outflows without harming relationships with suppliers, possibly by negotiating extended payment terms.

Optimizing the cash conversion cycle plays a crucial role here. This cycle analyzes the time span between outlaying cash for raw materials and receiving customer payment for the products sold. Shortening this cycle can significantly enhance your liquidity. Strategies include managing inventory more efficiently to avoid overstocking, speeding up production cycles, and tightening credit terms given to customers.

Tools for Cash Analogies

Leveraging tools and software for cash flow analysis is indispensable for keeping a vigilant eye on these aspects. Tools like QuickBooks, Xero, Sage, or even specialized cash flow management tools like Float can automate much of this tracking. They provide dashboards that offer a real-time snapshot of your financial status, highlighting how much cash is available, what's coming in, and what's going out. This real-time data is crucial for making informed financial decisions quickly.

These tools also allow for scenario planning and forecasting. You can test different business decisions to see how they would affect your cash flow. For instance, what happens if a major customer delays payment or a seasonal sales dip is lower than expected? Forecasting these scenarios allows you to prepare strategies to mitigate potential cash shortfalls.

Planning for Cash Flow Challenges

Despite best efforts, cash flow challenges can arise, often due to circumstances beyond your control such as economic downturns or unexpected large expenses. To safeguard against these, establishing lines of credit can provide a safety net. Unlike loans, lines of credit are flexible; you only use what you need, and you only pay interest on what you use. This can be crucial for bridging gaps when cash flow is tight.

Let's say you manufacture widgets. You sell an average of 1000 widgets a month at a price of $100 each, for gross sales of $100,000 per month. Your fixed costs (rent, utilities, salaries) are

$30,000 per month, and your variable costs (cost per unit) are $40 or $40,000 per month. You bill your customers on a net/30 basis, which means they have 30 days to pay the invoice you sent to them for the widgets. The following month your best customer triples his order. Now you have to pay for the raw materials for the new widgets yet have to wait 30 days to get paid by your customer. Will you be able to handle this new order?

A good cash flow spreadsheet will tell you exactly how much money you have coming in and when it should appear on the books. It will also tell you what you will need to pay for the additional materials and whether or not you will have enough cash available. Should you need to obtain additional funding then being able to show not only that you need the funds and how much, but exactly when you will need them, and more importantly when you will be able to pay them back can make the difference in whether or not you get approved for the additional funding.

Another wise strategy is to keep emergency funds. This involves setting aside a reserve of cash, built up during more profitable times, that can be used in a pinch.

Managing cash flow effectively is not just about keeping your business solvent; it's about ensuring it has the financial flexibility to seize opportunities and weather storms. By understanding and implementing strong cash flow management practices, you equip your business with the tools to maintain steady growth and long-term stability.

As this chapter closes, remember that managing your business's finances is a dynamic, ongoing process that requires continuous attention and adjustment. The strategies discussed here are not one-time tasks but part of an ongoing effort to improve your business's financial health.

THREE

Building Your Brand and Marketing

Stepping into the marketplace without a distinct brand is like walking into a major conference without a name tag—no one knows who you are, and you might just blend into the crowd. Your brand is your promise to your customer. It tells them what they can expect from your products and services and differentiates your offerings from those of your competitors. Think of your brand as your unique signature—it's not just a logo or a set of colors but the complete experience your customers have with your company. So, how do you ensure your brand takes center stage and captivates the audience? Let's dive into developing a strong brand identity, the cornerstone of any effective marketing strategy.

3.1 Developing a Strong Brand Identity: Logos, Colors, and More

Importance of Visual Identity

Visual identity goes beyond aesthetics; it communicates your business's values and promises at a glance. A well-crafted logo, a consistent color scheme, and professional typography can create a sense of trust and quality in your customers' minds. For instance, think about the last time you chose a product off the shelf, perhaps influenced by a recognizable logo or color that you associated with quality. That's visual identity at work. It's about using visual elements to make your brand memorable and distinguishable in a sea of competitors.

Your logo should serve as the cornerstone of your brand identity. It's the face of your company and often the first thing customers will notice. Therefore, it must encapsulate your brand's essence and be easily recognizable. Color schemes also play a pivotal role; different colors evoke different feelings and associations. For example, blue can evoke trust and dependability, while green is often associated with health and sustainability. Typography, meanwhile, can influence how readable and perceivable your content is. The suitable typeface should communicate your brand's character and ensure legibility across various mediums.

Design Principles

When it comes to design, simplicity, consistency, and relevance are your guiding principles. A simple design isn't just about minimalism; it's about clarity and focus. It ensures your brand is easily recognized and remembered. Consistency across all platforms, from your website to your packaging, reinforces your brand identity and helps forge a cohesive brand image. Every element, from your logo to your font choices, should be consistent in style and aligned with the overall character of your brand, reinforcing who you are as a company.

Relevance is equally crucial. Your visual elements should not only be appealing but also appropriate for your audience. For instance, a tech startup might opt for a sleek, modern font and a clean, minimalist logo to convey innovation and efficiency. On the other hand, a children's toy company might choose bright colors and a playful font to appeal to its young audience.

Choosing the Right Design Tools

Not everyone can afford a professional graphic designer, but that doesn't mean your brand identity must suffer. Numerous user-friendly design tools can help you create professional-looking logos and branding materials. Canva, for example, offers a range of templates that you can customize to fit your brand. Adobe Spark and LogoMakr are other tools that provide flexibility and ease of use, allowing even those with minimal design experience to create eye-catching logos.

These tools often provide tutorials and templates that are informed by fundamental design principles, ensuring that even novices can create visually appealing and effective designs. Additionally, they are generally cost-effective, some even offering free basic services, making them ideal for bootstrapped startups.

Legal Considerations

While crafting your visual identity, it's crucial to ensure that your designs are not only striking but also legally sound. This means conducting thorough trademark searches for your logo and brand name to ensure they aren't already in use. The last thing you want is a legal challenge from another business claiming that your logo or brand name infringes on their trademark. Websites like the U.S. Patent and Trademark Office provide resources where you can conduct these searches.

Furthermore, when using design tools or hiring designers, ensure that any elements used (like icons or photographs) are either original or correctly licensed. Copyright infringement can lead to hefty fines and legal battles, which can be particularly damaging for a new business. Always check the licensing agreements of any assets you use to ensure that you have the right to use them in your commercial endeavors.

Creating a strong brand identity isn't just about looking good—it's about being remembered, conveying your values, and connecting with your audience visually. By focusing on creating a consistent, simple, and relevant visual identity and ensuring all legal bases are covered, you can build a brand that truly stands out. With the right tools and a careful approach, your brand's visual identity will not only capture attention but also win hearts, setting the foundation for lasting customer relationships.

3.2 Building an Online Presence: Websites and Social Media Basics

Creating a robust online presence is akin to building a digital storefront. It's where your customers come to window shop, learn more about your offerings, and decide whether they want to walk through the door. So, what makes a business website effective? It begins with a few essential components. First, your homepage should grab attention and clearly communicate what your business is; what you do and who you are. Think of it as your digital handshake—first impressions matter. It should have a clean, attractive design and easy navigation so that visitors can find what they're looking for without hassle.

Next up is your 'About' page. Here's where you tell your brand's story. Share what drives you, your business's history, and what differentiates you from the competition. This page is your opportunity to connect on a more personal level with your customers and make your business relatable. Then, ensure your 'Contact' information is easy to find and use.

Lastly, if you're selling products or services directly from your site, each product or service should have its own detailed page. High-quality images, comprehensive descriptions, specifications, and prices should be clearly presented. Each product/service page should effectively communicate what the customer is getting, why it's worth their money, and how they can purchase it.

Let's switch gears to social media. This is where you can significantly start to grow your audience and engage directly with customers. But not all platforms are created equal, and not every platform will be suitable for your business. Selecting the right platforms depends primarily on where your target audience spends their time. For instance, if your target market includes professionals, LinkedIn could be a great choice. If your business is highly visual, like a clothing brand or a bakery, Instagram and Pinterest could be more appropriate.

Once you've chosen the most suitable platforms the next step is engagement. This means more than just posting regularly; it also means interacting with your followers, responding to comments, and participating in community discussions. Sharing behind-the-scenes content, running live Q&A sessions, and offering special promotions are all effective ways to engage your audience. Remember, social media is a two-way street; the more you engage with your audience, the more they will engage with your brand.

Integrating e-commerce into your website can transform your digital presence from an informational hub to a revenue-generating machine. The first step is choosing the right e-commerce platform. Options such as Shopify, WooCommerce, or BigCommerce offer various features based on different needs, such as digital products, subscriptions, or international sales. Each platform has its strengths, so consider your specific needs and technical capabilities before deciding.

Payment gateways are another critical element. They need to be secure and reliable. Options such as PayPal, Stripe, and Square are popular because of their robust security measures and ease of integration. Remember, the smoother the payment process, the less likely customers are to abandon their carts.

Security is non-negotiable in e-commerce. Implementing SSL certificates to encrypt data, ensuring compliance with PCI DSS standards, and using secure passwords and authentication methods are all essential steps to protecting your customers' information.

Lastly, the power of analytics in digital marketing cannot be overstated. Tools like Google Analytics for your website or insights from social media platforms provide valuable data about who your visitors are, how they interact with your content, and what strategies drive the most engagement and sales. This data is crucial for refining your marketing strategies. It allows you to see what's working, what isn't, and where you can improve. Regularly reviewing these analytics should be a key part of your strategy, guiding your decisions and helping you to better understand your audience.

3.3 Content Marketing for Startups: Creating Engaging Content That Converts

In the realm of digital marketing, content is more than just king—it's the ace, the joker, and the queen all rolled into one. It's the vehicle that carries your brand's voice straight into the hearts and minds of your audience. But not all content is created equal. To truly resonate with your target audience and achieve your business goals, you need a solid plan that aligns with your brand ethos and meets the needs of your market. Here's where a well-crafted content calendar comes into play. Think of it like planning out your meals for the week—you decide beforehand what to cook, ensuring you have all the ingredients ready and avoiding last-minute unhealthy choices. Similarly, a content calendar helps you organize themes, important dates, and content release schedules, ensuring your content is thoughtful, timely, and, most importantly, strategic.

Start by identifying key dates important to your industry—major holidays, industry-specific events, or product launch dates. These are your anchor points. Next, fill in the blanks with content that educates, entertains, or inspires your audience, keeping them engaged and connected to your brand. For instance, if you run an online fashion store, align your content with fashion weeks, seasonal changes, or celebrity style news, providing your audience with fresh, relevant content that sparks interest and engagement.

Now, let's talk about the variety of content formats available. Blogs are a fantastic way to delve deep into topics, showcase your expertise, and improve your SEO rankings. Conversely, videos are incredibly engaging and can give your audience a quick, visually appealing insight into your products or services. Infographics are great for breaking down complex information into digestible, shareable visuals. At the same time, podcasts can capture the attention of those in your audience who prefer audio content, perhaps during their commute or workout.

Each format serves a different purpose and has its place in your content strategy. For example, blogs are perfect for detailed how-tos or thought leadership articles, while videos might be better for product demos or behind-the-scenes looks at your business. The key is to understand what your audience prefers and what will best convey your message.

When creating content, remember that quality trumps quantity every time. High-quality content is more likely to get shared, increasing your visibility and enhancing your reputation as a trustworthy source. To ensure quality, focus on creating original content that adds real value. Use SEO strategies like incorporating relevant keywords naturally into your content, but always prioritize readability and engagement over keyword stuffing. Storytelling is another powerful technique—people remember stories much better than facts. Share customer success stories, the history of your company, or even day-to-day experiences that your audience can relate to. This makes your content more engaging and strengthens your brand's connection with your audience.

Finally, let's talk about turning readers and viewers into customers —optimizing content for conversions. Content should have a clear, compelling call to action (CTA). Whether it's encouraging readers to sign up for a newsletter, share the content on social media, or make a purchase, your CTA should be obvious and easy to follow. Landing pages are critical here; they should match the promise made in the content and make the conversion process as simple and straightforward as possible. For instance, if your blog post is about the benefits of a particular product, link directly to a landing page where readers can purchase the product. Content upgrades, such as free ebooks, checklists, or webinars, can also be effective. Offer these in exchange for contact details, allowing you to nurture leads through more personalized content.

By planning your content strategically, choosing the proper formats, focusing on quality creation, and optimizing for conversions, you can transform your content marketing from a scattershot of posts and videos into a targeted, powerful tool that drives business growth and builds meaningful relationships with your audience. Make your content work not just harder but smarter, and watch as it becomes a key player in your business's success story.

3.4 Utilizing SEO for Business Growth: Tactics for Beginners

Navigating the maze of Search Engine Optimization (SEO) might seem daunting at first, but understanding the basics can significantly improve your online visibility and drive more traffic to your website. At its core, SEO is about enhancing your website's presence in search engine results, making it easier for potential customers to find you when they search for products or services related to your business. Let's start with the fundamentals: search engines like Google use algorithms to determine the relevance and quality of your site for specific keywords. These are the terms and phrases that people type into the search bar when they're looking for information.

The first step in mastering SEO is to identify the right keywords for your business. Think about what potential customers might search for when looking for your products or services. Tools like Google Keyword Planner or Moz Keyword Explorer can help you find keywords related to your business and see how often they are searched. Once you have a list of keywords, the challenge is to integrate them naturally into your website's content. This includes your web pages, blog posts, titles, and meta descriptions. But remember, stuffing your content with too many keywords can lead to a penalty from search engines, so using them thoughtfully and naturally is essential.

Meta tags, including title tags and meta descriptions, also play a critical role in SEO. These elements provide search engines with a snapshot of what your page is about. Your title tag is the clickable headline that appears in search results, and it should include your main keyword if possible. The meta description, on the other hand, provides a brief summary of the page content and is your chance to entice users to click through to your website. Both should be compelling, include relevant keywords, and fit within the character limits that search engines display.

Backlinks, or links from other websites to yours, are also crucial for SEO. They act like votes of confidence from other sites, indicating to search engines that your content is valuable and trustworthy. However, not all backlinks are created equal. Links from high-authority websites will have a greater impact on your SEO than those from low-quality sites. To build backlinks, consider creating shareable content that other websites will want to link to, or engage in guest blogging on reputable sites in your industry.

On-page SEO Techniques

Once you've got a handle on keywords and meta tags, it's time to dive deeper into on-page SEO techniques. These are adjustments you make directly to your website's content and structure to improve its performance in search rankings. First, focus on optimizing your titles and descriptions to catch the user's eye and include relevant keywords. Next, look at your content structure. Breaking your content into smaller paragraphs with headings helps make it more digestible for readers. It allows you to use your keywords effectively in headings, further enhancing your SEO.

Also, consider your website's URL structure. URLs should be simple, understandable, and include keywords if possible. For example, if you sell organic coffee, a URL like www.yourdomain.com/organic-arabica-coffee is much more SEO-friendly than www.yourdomain.com/product-item123456. Additionally, optimizing images is crucial. Large images can slow down your site, negatively affecting your search engine rankings. Compress images and include alt text with relevant keywords, which helps search engines understand what the image depicts.

Local SEO

For small businesses, local SEO can be a game-changer. It focuses on optimizing your online presence to attract more business from relevant local searches. The most critical tool for local SEO is your Google My Business profile. This free listing allows you to appear in local search results and Google Maps, providing potential customers with essential information like your business hours, location, and services. To optimize your profile, ensure all your information is accurate and up-to-date, add photos of your business, and encourage customers to leave reviews.

Local keywords should also be a part of your SEO strategy. These are terms that include specific locations. For example, "coffee shop in Austin" or "best organic coffee near downtown Austin." Including these keywords in your content can help you rank higher in local search results. Additionally, embedding a Google Map on your contact page and using local business schema markup can further enhance your local SEO efforts.

Monitoring SEO Progress

Lastly, tracking your SEO progress is vital for understanding what's working and what needs adjustment. Tools like Google Analytics and Google Search Console can provide valuable insights into your traffic, how users find your site, and which pages are the most popular. These tools can also help you monitor your site's health, track your rankings, and understand how users interact with your content.

Regular monitoring allows you to refine your SEO strategies and make data-driven decisions to improve your site's performance. Remember, SEO is not a set-it-and-forfeit endeavor; it requires ongoing adjustments and updates to keep up with changes in search engine algorithms and shifts in consumer behavior. By staying proactive and responsive, you can ensure that your SEO efforts drive meaningful results, helping your business grow and thrive in the digital marketplace.

3.5 Low-Budget Marketing Strategies with High Impact

Effective marketing doesn't necessarily mean breaking the bank in today's hyper-competitive business landscape. There are numerous ingenious low-cost marketing tactics that can significantly amplify your visibility and help you carve out a niche without exhausting your budget. Let's explore some captivating guerilla marketing tactics, which are all about creativity and making a big splash with minimal investment. Guerilla marketing is essentially an advertising strategy that focuses on low-cost unconventional marketing tactics that yield maximum results. This approach is about taking people by surprise, making a real impression, and creating copious amounts of social buzz.

Imagine using sidewalk chalk to draw a path leading to your cafe or setting up a pop-up event in a local park showcasing your products. These tactics not only draw attention but also create a memorable experience for potential customers. Another low-cost guerilla tactic could involve assembling large-scale art installations in public places related to your product. If you're selling eco-friendly products, you might create an art piece from recycled materials and display it downtown with a sign about your business. The key here is to think outside the box and develop scenarios that encourage interaction and naturally lead to sharing on social media.

Leveraging community resources is another splendid way to boost your business's profile without a hefty price tag. Participate in local events or team up with other local businesses for joint promotions. This not only increases your visibility but also helps build your local network, which can be invaluable. Community boards, both physical and digital, offer free spaces to post information about your services and events. Similarly, partnerships with other local businesses can lead to collaborative events, such as workshops or festivals, which can draw crowds and media attention without the cost of solo advertising.

Email marketing remains one of the most cost-effective marketing strategies available. For the price of a decent email platform subscription, you can reach hundreds or even thousands of potential customers. The key to successful email marketing is building and maintaining an effective email list. Offer incentives for customers to sign up, like discounts or freebies, and keep them engaged with regular updates, exclusive offers, and valuable content that keeps them opening your emails. Tools like MailChimp or Constant Contact provide user-friendly platforms that allow you to design, send, and track emails effectively, ensuring that you're not just sending messages into the void.

Social media advertising can be another economical way to increase your business's online presence and attract new customers. Platforms like Facebook, Instagram, and X (formerly-Twitter) offer powerful targeting options that allow you to reach specific demographics at a relatively low cost. The key is to create compelling content that resonates with your audience—be it through eye-catching images, engaging videos, or insightful posts. Start small, with a modest budget, and use the detailed analytics these platforms provide to see what works best. For example, you might run several versions of an ad to see which image or headline draws more clicks, then invest more in the most effective version.

Each of these strategies requires creativity more than capital. With a bit of ingenuity, you can implement marketing tactics that not only saves money but also makes your business stand out in a crowded market that keeps your customers returning.

3.6 Networking and Partnerships: Growing Your Business Community

In the hustle of setting up and running a business, take notice of the immense value hidden within professional networks and strategic partnerships. Think of your business as part of a broader ecosystem, where connections can open doors to new opportunities, provide essential business advice, and significantly amplify your reach. Effective networking isn't just about collecting business cards; it's about cultivating meaningful relationships that can lead to mutual growth and success.

Firstly, let's unpack the art of networking. Whether at industry conferences, local business meetups, or online forums, your goal is to be more than just present. You need to engage. Start by setting clear objectives for what you want to achieve from each event—be it finding a mentor, identifying potential business partners, or gaining insights into market trends. When you meet new people, focus on how you can help them. This approach not only makes you memorable but also sets the stage for reciprocal assistance. Remember, effective networking is a two-way street.

Utilizing digital tools has also revolutionized how we connect with others. Platforms like LinkedIn allow you to reach out to industry leaders and peers irrespective of geographical boundaries. Participate actively in relevant LinkedIn groups, share your insights, and comment on posts by others to boost your visibility and establish your expertise. However, balance is key. While online networking can extend your reach, face-to-face interactions often build deeper connections. Maintain a blend of both to maximize your networking effectiveness.

Next, let's dive into the world of strategic partnerships. These alliances can be a game-changer, especially for businesses looking to expand their market reach or enhance their service offerings. The first step is to identify potential partners who complement your business. This could be a company that offers products or services that align with yours or one that shares your target market but isn't a direct competitor. For instance, if you own a wedding photography business, partnering with local florists or event planners could be beneficial. Each party can refer clients to the other, creating a win-win situation.

Engaging with your local community is another powerful strategy. Community engagement goes beyond mere brand exposure; it builds brand loyalty and trust. This could involve sponsoring local sports teams, participating in community clean-up days, or hosting educational workshops. Each of these activities demonstrates your business's commitment to the community and can lead to natural, positive publicity. Moreover, community engagement often leads to genuine connections with potential customers and local influencers who can advocate for your brand.

Lastly, tapping into business associations can provide additional networking opportunities and resources. These organizations bring together businesses from various sectors, offering a platform for sharing knowledge, resources, and support. They often host regular meetings, workshops, and seminars that can keep you updated on industry trends and best practices. Membership can also lend credibility to your business, as these associations often have stringent standards for quality and reliability.

There are organizations set up expressly for this purpose. One such organization is Business Networking International (BNI). You can find local chapters set up near you. Each chapter consists of a number of members of different business types, and each chapter admits only one member of each kind of business. You may have a chapter near you that consists of one banker, one insurance agent, one electrician, one plumber, one business consultant and/or coach, one financial planner, one landscaper, etc. Not only do they work among themselves, they serve as a source of references for others within the group. For example, an insurance agent might be meeting with a couple who have recently purchased a home. In the course of supplying the needed insurance the couple mentions that they are having trouble with the water draining very slowly in the bath in the back part of the home. The agent lets them know that he can have an associate (a fellow BNI member) who has his own plumbing company give them a call the following day. A group of 30-40 business owners each supplying references for each other can be a powerful tool to obtain new business. Another networking site that should not be overlooked is your local chamber of commerce. These chambers have networking events regularly for their members to promote their business to other members and to exchange references.

By actively engaging in networking, forging strategic partnerships, participating in your community, and leveraging business associations, you can significantly enhance your business's visibility, credibility, and market reach. Each connection you make is a potential gateway to new opportunities, ready to elevate your business to new heights.

As we wrap up this chapter on building your brand and marketing, remember the power of relationships in business. Your network can propel you forward, your partnerships can open new avenues, and your community engagement can solidify your brand's presence.

FOUR

Sales Strategies and Customer Management

I magine you're at a bustling county fair. Everywhere you look booths are vying for your attention, each with their own gimmicks, games, and giveaways. Now, picture your business there. How do you turn the heads of passersby, draw them into your booth, and convert their curiosity into sales? That's where mastering your sales funnel comes into play. It's not just about grabbing attention; it's about guiding that initial interest through to a decision and action. In this chapter, we'll break down the sales funnel stages and show you how to tailor one that resonates with both your business's essence and customer behavior, ensuring that from first glance to final purchase, your business is the main attraction.

4.1 Setting Up Your Sales Funnel: A Beginner's Guide

Understanding the Sales Funnel Stages

A sales funnel is structured into several key stages—Awareness, Interest, Decision, and Action (AIDA). Each stage represents a different level of engagement with your potential customer. Initially, in the Awareness stage, you're making potential customers aware of your solution. This could be through social media posts, blogs, or even word of mouth. The key here is to cast a wide net, grabbing the attention of as many potential customers as possible.

Moving down the funnel, we reach the Interest stage. Your potential customers know about you; now it's about piquing their interest. This is where targeted content, such as newsletters, eBooks, or more in-depth blog posts, comes into play. You're not just telling them that your product exists; you're explaining why it matters.

As we delve deeper, the Decision stage is next. Here, potential customers are considering whether to purchase your product or service. They might be comparing your offerings with competitors, reviewing pricing, or checking testimonials. Your job is to sway their decision in your favor with great offers, compelling case studies, or irresistible guarantees.

Finally, the Action stage is where the purchase happens. But your interaction shouldn't stop there. Encouraging repeat business and referrals by following up, asking for feedback, and offering post-purchase support is crucial in turning a one-time buyer into a loyal customer.

Designing Your Sales Funnel

Designing an effective sales funnel requires a deep understanding of your product and market, but most importantly, an understanding of your customer's behavior and needs. Start by mapping out the customer journey. What does your typical customer look like? What are their pain points, and how does your product solve these issues? Each stage of your funnel should be designed to smoothly transition them from one stage to the next, gently nudging them towards a purchase.

For instance, if you're selling a high-tech gadget, your awareness content might be tech blogs and social media posts that highlight the latest advancements in technology. Interest could be piqued by in-depth videos explaining the gadget's unique features. Decisions could be swayed by side-by-side comparisons with other gadgets, and action can be facilitated with an easy, hassle-free online purchasing process.

Tools for Funnel Creation

Several tools can help in crafting and managing your sales funnel. Customer Relationship Management (CRM) systems like Salesforce, HubSpot, or Bigin can track your interactions with potential and current customers, helping you understand where each person is in the funnel and how best to address their needs. Email marketing software, such as Mailchimp or Constant Contact, is crucial for automating parts of the funnel, like sending targeted emails that nudge potential customers from one stage to the next.

Analyzing and Optimizing the Funnel

Once your funnel is in operation, constant analysis and optimization are key. Use analytics to track how customers are moving through your funnel. Where are the drop-off points? At what stage are you losing potential customers? Tools like Google Analytics can help you track these metrics. A/B testing different approaches can also tell you what's working and what's not. Does one landing page convert better than another, or does a particular email subject line get more opens? Use this data to refine your funnel continually.

Effective sales funnel management is dynamic. It addresses insights and refinements based on real-time data and customer feedback. By understanding each stage of the funnel and continuously enhancing it, you can significantly boost your conversion rates and, ultimately, your bottom line. Remember, a great sales funnel isn't just about capturing sales; it's about creating a seamless, enjoyable journey that leaves customers eager to return and engage even further with your brand.

4.2 Effective Pricing Strategies: Finding the Sweet Only Spot

When you set the price for your products or services, you're not just putting a number on a tag; you're communicating value, positioning yourself in the market, and directly affecting your ability to make a profit. Let's walk through some of the critical strategies to ensure your pricing not only covers your costs but also captures the value you provide to your customers, keeping you competitive and adaptable in ever-changing market conditions.

Cost-Based Pricing

Starting with the basics, cost-based pricing is like ensuring every slice of the pie costs enough to pay for the ingredients and the chef's time, with a little extra left over as profit. To implement this strategy, you first need to tally up the cost of goods sold (COGS), which includes every expense directly involved in production—from raw materials to the labor used in assembly. But that's not all; you also need to consider the overall business costs—such as rent, utilities, and salaries for employees not directly involved in production. Once you have a total, add a markup percentage that represents your desired profit margin. This percentage can vary significantly depending on your industry, market position, and brand perception. A common mistake is setting this markup without a clear rationale, which can either lead to prices that scare away potential customers or leave money on the table. A good practice is to analyze how similar products are priced in your industry and adjust your markup based on your competitive advantages or unique selling propositions..

Margin vs. Markup-What Is The Difference

Cost-based pricing is usually calculated one of two ways: by using either "margin" or by using "markup". How are these different?

You decide that adding a new item to your inventory to sell would be advantageous. These new items cost you $100 apiece to purchase. Let's calculate the retail price under each method.

Markup is simply what it says. You take the cost and mark it up by a certain percentage or dollar amount. If you want a 40% markup, the retail price would be $100 + $40 (40% of $100) for a total price of $140.00.

Many businesses prefer to price according to margin.

Margin is calculated based on the profit that will be made. Using the same $100 item, we now want a 40% margin, or 40% profit on the item.

To calculate margin you would subtract the amount of profit (40% or .4) from 100, which leaves 60% (or .6). Then divide the cost ($100) by the remaining decimal (.6) to get the retail price, which here would be $166.67. This is a 40% margin, as $66.67 is 40% of $166.67.

As you can see, a 40% markup is only a 28.6% margin ($40 divided by $140).

To summarize, markup is calculated on the cost of the item, whereas margin is calculated based on the retail price of the item.

Value-Based Pricing

Switching gears, value-based pricing is less about the cost of the pie and more about how much someone is willing to pay for it based on their perceived value. This strategy requires a deep understanding of your customer's needs and how they measure value. Are they paying for luxury, convenience, durability, or a combination of these? Factors that can affect perceived value include brand reputation, product quality, customer service, and even social responsibility practices. To enhance perceived value, consider improving product design, offering exceptional customer experiences, or aligning your brand with socially conscious initiatives, which can justify higher price points. The key here is communication. Your marketing efforts should clearly articulate the benefits and reasons why your product is worth a premium, helping customers understand and appreciate the value they're getting for their money.

Competitive Pricing Analysis

Keeping an eye on the competition is crucial when setting prices. Competitive pricing analysis involves gathering data on how similar products or services are priced in the market. This doesn't mean you should match or beat those prices, but it helps you understand where you stand. Are you positioned as a budget-friendly option or are you aiming for the premium end of the spectrum? Tools like price tracking software can automate this process, providing real-time data on competitor pricing strategies. With this information, you can make informed decisions about whether to adjust your prices. You may find a gap in the market for a mid-priced product, or you may discover that you can increase your prices without affecting demand. Remember, the goal isn't just to compete on price but to strategically position your pricing to align with your business goals and brand identity.

Dynamic Pricing Techniques

Imagine if you could adjust your prices on the fly, responding in real time to changes in demand, market conditions, or competitive actions. That's dynamic pricing, a strategy often used by airlines and hotels but increasingly applicable in various sectors thanks to modern e-commerce platforms and pricing algorithms. This technique allows you to maximize profits by raising prices during high-demand periods and lowering them when demand wanes, helping keep your inventory moving. Implementing dynamic pricing requires sophisticated software that can analyze large datasets and automate price adjustments. While this approach offers flexibility and potential revenue increases, it also demands transparency to maintain customer trust. Sudden price changes can lead to perceptions of price gouging if not managed carefully. Therefore, it's crucial to ensure that your dynamic pricing strategy is always aligned with providing value and maintaining a positive customer experience.

4.3 Customer Relationship Management: Tools and Techniques

Navigating the landscape of Customer Relationship Management (CRM) systems can sometimes feel like being a kid in a candy store. There are so many options, each promising to be the sweetest. But the right CRM system is more than just a treat; it's a fundamental tool that transforms how you interact with your customers, streamline your operations, and boost your sales. The trick is choosing one that fits not just your business's current size but also takes into account its future growth, aligning with your budget and specific needs. When selecting a CRM, start by assessing the scalability and integration capabilities. A good CRM should grow with your business, handling increasing data without hitches. It should also seamlessly integrate with your existing tools —be it your email platforms, accounting software, or customer service applications—creating a unified system that enhances efficiency rather than complicating it.

Furthermore, consider the CRM's usability. It should have a user-friendly interface that your team can adopt without needing extensive training. Advanced features are beneficial, but not if they overwhelm your users, leading to underutilization of the system. CRM systems like Salesforce and HubSpot are popular for their robust features and scalability. In contrast, systems like Zoho, Bigin, and Insightly are praised for their cost-effectiveness and ease of use, particularly suitable for small to mid-sized businesses.

Once you've selected the perfect CRM, integrating it into your daily operations is your next step. This integration is crucial as it ensures the CRM serves its purpose—enhancing your interactions with customers and streamlining your processes. Start by importing all your customer data into the system, ensuring it's clean and organized. This might involve some data cleanup, like removing duplicates or outdated information, which ensures your CRM's effectiveness. Next, set up features that match your business processes, such as sales pipelines, reporting tools, and customer segmentation. It's like setting up different rooms in a new home, each designated for a specific purpose, ensuring smooth daily operations.

Training your team is equally important. Even the best CRM can become a white elephant if your team doesn't know how to use it effectively. Provide comprehensive training that not only covers the technical aspects of the software but also how it fits into your overall sales and customer service strategies.

Leveraging CRM for Marketing and Sales

Using your CRM data to boost your marketing and sales efforts can be likened to a chef using their finest ingredients to create a signature dish. The data your CRM collects—customer preferences, purchase history, interaction logs, etc—is a goldmine of insights that can significantly enhance your marketing campaigns and sales strategies. Use this data to segment your customers based on various criteria like demographics, behavior, and purchase history. This segmentation allows for more targeted and personalized marketing efforts. For instance, you can send customized email campaigns that address individual customer's preferences, which can increase engagement and conversion rates.

CRM data helps you identify potential upsell or cross-sell opportunities, improving customer lifetime value and increasing sales. It also enables sales teams to track their interactions with potential leads, ensuring timely follow-ups that can make the difference between a sale and a missed opportunity. Moreover, integrating your CRM with marketing automation tools can streamline the lead nurturing process, automatically sending personalized messages and content that move leads down the sales funnel more efficiently.

Measuring CRM Success

To truly understand the impact of your CRM, you need to measure its success using specific metrics. These metrics give you a clear picture of how the CRM is contributing to your business goals. Key performance indicators (KPIs) such as customer retention rates, customer lifetime value, lead conversion rates, and sales cycle lengths are crucial. For example, an increase in customer retention rates might indicate that your CRM-driven service improvements are resonating with your customers. Similarly, a decrease in sales cycle lengths could suggest that your CRM's lead management features are effectively streamlining your sales processes.

Regularly reviewing these KPIs helps you gauge the effectiveness of your CRM and identify areas for improvement. It's about continuously refining your processes and strategies based on data-driven insights, ensuring that your CRM investment is not just justified, but is actively driving business growth.

To summarize, a well-chosen and effectively integrated CRM system can revolutionize how you manage customer relationships and drive your sales efforts. It's about turning data into actionable insights that not only streamline your operations but also enhance your interactions with customers, paving the way for sustained business growth and success.

4.4 Handling Objections and Closing Deals: A Step-by-Step Approach

When you're in the thick of sales discussions, objections are as common as morning coffee. Think of them not as roadblocks but as opportunities to deepen your understanding of your client's needs and refine your sales pitch. Whether it's a concern over price, uncertainty about product capabilities, or just old-fashioned indecision, your ability to handle these objections gracefully can make or break a deal.

Identifying Common Objections

First, let's talk about identifying those common objections you're likely to encounter. For example, if you're selling software solutions, common objections may include concerns about integration with existing systems, the complexity of use, or even the ROI it delivers. In retail, objections often revolve around price, product need, or quality assurance. The best way to prepare is by having a deep understanding of both your product and your customer. This means you should not only know every nut and bolt of what you're selling but also have a clear picture of your customer's industry, their pain points, and their common hurdles. This dual insight allows you to anticipate objections and prepare clear, compelling responses that address them directly.

Strategies to Overcome Objections

Overcoming objections is an art form that requires patience, empathy, and a good dose of strategic thinking. One effective technique is the "feel, felt, found" method. Here's how it works: when a client presents an objection, first validate their concern (feel), then share a credible anecdote of a similar past scenario where another client had a similar concern (felt), and conclude by telling them how your product or service provided a solution (found). For instance, if a client is worried about the cost of your service, you might respond with, "I understand why you feel that the investment is substantial. Many of our clients initially felt the same way. However, they found that the increase in their operational efficiency actually lowered overall costs within a few months." This method not only shows empathy but also builds credibility and trust, helping to ease concerns by illustrating how others have successfully navigated similar challenges.

Another key strategy is to refine your questioning techniques. The goal here is to understand the underlying reasons for objections. Sometimes what seems like a cost issue is actually about value perception. By asking open-ended questions, you can uncover deeper concerns and address them directly.

Closing Techniques

Now, let's pivot to closing techniques, which vary widely depending on the situation and customer type. One classic method is the "assumptive close," where you act as if the client has already decided to purchase, and you move forward with discussing the next steps. This could be as simple as saying, "So, would Tuesday or Wednesday be better for delivery?" This technique works well when a client needs just a gentle nudge to make a decision.

Another effective approach is the "summary close," where you recap all the agreed-upon points and benefits, reinforcing the value before asking for the sale. This not only reminds the client of why they were interested in the first place but also minimizes the impact of any lingering objections by putting them in context with all the benefits.

Follow-Up Strategies

Finally, effective follow-up strategies are crucial for sealing the deal, especially when it doesn't close immediately. The key here is persistence and timing. A follow-up schedule might look like an email the day after the meeting, a phone call a week later, and then periodic check-ins every few weeks. Each interaction should add value by providing additional information that addresses ongoing concerns or just checking in to maintain the relationship. Tools like CRM systems can automate much of this process, ensuring you keep potential deals from slipping through the cracks due to poor follow-up.

Remember, each client is unique; thus, every sales conversation is different. Flexibility and adaptability are your best assets when it comes to handling objections and closing deals. By understanding common objections, employing strategic techniques to overcome them, and using effective closing and follow-up strategies, you'll not only increase your sales success rate but also build stronger, more enduring relationships with your clients.

4.5 Building Customer Loyalty: Programs and Practices That Work

Creating a sustainable business isn't just about finding new customers—it's about keeping the ones you already have and turning them into avid supporters of your brand. Developing robust customer loyalty programs is an essential part of your business strategy that can significantly boost your bottom line. Think about it: it's much more cost-effective to sell to an existing customer than to acquire a new one. Loyalty programs, when done right, provide a compelling reason for customers to keep returning. They can take many forms, from point systems that reward customers for purchases to VIP benefits for your most loyal patrons. For instance, consider a point system where customers earn points for each purchase, which they can later redeem for discounts, special products, or exclusive experiences. This not only encourages repeat purchases but also makes the shopping experience more engaging.

VIP benefits add another layer to your loyalty strategy. These may include early access to new products, special members-only discounts, or even invitations to private events. These perks make customers feel valued and unique, strengthening their emotional connection to your brand. Exclusive offers can also be a great way to keep your customer base engaged. For example, offering a special discount on a customer's birthday is a personal touch that makes someone feel appreciated. It's these thoughtful details that transform occasional customers into loyal fans.

Beyond rewards and perks, personalization plays a crucial role in modern customer loyalty strategies. With the wealth of data available, you can tailor your communications and offers to fit your customers' individual preferences and behaviors. Personalization isn't just about addressing an email to someone by their first name —it's about providing relevant recommendations and content that resonate with their specific needs and desires. For example, if a customer frequently buys organic products from your store, sending them information on new additions to your organic range can be a highly effective strategy. It shows you understand and value their preferences.

Customer appreciation is another vital element. Simple gestures like sending thank you notes or reaching out with personalized messages can make customers feel valued. Events, whether online or in person, also offer a dynamic way to engage with your customer base and show appreciation. These can range from product launch parties to customer appreciation days where loyal customers can avail themselves of exclusive deals.

Feedback loops are essential for continuous improvement and can significantly enhance customer satisfaction. Inviting customers to provide feedback after a purchase or a service experience helps you gather valuable insights into what works and what doesn't. This feedback can be leveraged to make improvements to your products or services. Implementing a simple, accessible way for customers to give feedback, such as through an online form or a quick survey at the end of a chat session, can provide you with ongoing insights. Moreover, showing customers that their feedback has led to real changes enhances their trust and loyalty, as they feel their opinions actually matter.

Building a community around your brand can further enhance customer loyalty. This involves creating spaces, either online or physical, where customers can interact with each other and your brand. Social media platforms, forums, and user groups are excellent for fostering this sense of community. Regularly engaging with these communities by responding to comments, sharing insider tips, or asking for input on new products can make customers feel part of something bigger. This is particularly effective for brands with a strong lifestyle component, where customers share common interests or values.

In essence, building customer loyalty is about creating an ecosystem around your brand where customers receive continuous value not just from the products or services they purchase but also from their overall experience with your brand, turning casual customers into loyal advocates who will help your business thrive in the long run.

4.6 Expanding Your Market Reach: When and How to Scale

Scaling your business is like hitting the open road after you've learned to drive: it's thrilling and full of opportunities, but without a map and some sensible planning, you might find yourself off course. The first step in scaling is identifying new market opportunities. This could mean exploring new geographic regions, tapping into different demographic groups, or extending your product line to include complementary items or services. Start by analyzing market data and trends to spot potential areas of growth. Look for underserved markets or regions where your competitors are not active. Social listening tools and customer feedback can also provide insights into what new products or features your customers are seeking.

Once you've pinpointed where you want to expand, consider the logistical aspects of scaling your sales operations. This includes ensuring you have the right team in place. Scaling usually requires more hands on deck, so assess your current team's capacity and determine if additional staff or training is necessary. Remember, maintaining your company culture and service standards is crucial as your team grows. Training programs for new hires should not only cover job skills but also instill your business's values and customer service philosophy.

Expanding sales channels is another critical element. If you're a retail business, this might mean opening new store locations or setting up pop-up shops in high-traffic areas. For service-based businesses, consider expanding your online presence or partnering with other companies to offer your services. E-commerce platforms can also provide new avenues for product sales. Each channel comes with its own set of challenges, so it's essential to tailor your approach based on the channel's specific demands and customer expectations.

When reaching these new markets, digital marketing is an invaluable tool. Leveraging social media advertising can help you precisely target specific geographic or demographic markets. Platforms like Facebook and Instagram offer advanced targeting options based on location, age, interests, and more, allowing you to reach potential customers most likely interested in your products. Conversely, content marketing helps establish your brand's authority and reach an audience looking for information. By creating valuable content that addresses the needs and questions of your target market, you can attract, engage, and convert new customers. For instance, if you're expanding into a younger demographic, short, engaging video content on platforms like TikTok or YouTube might be more effective than traditional long-form articles.

Managing Risk in Scaling

As you shift into expansion mode, managing the risks associated with scaling is essential. One common mistake is scaling too quickly without proper groundwork, which can strain resources and affect service quality. To mitigate this, develop a phased scaling plan that allows you to increase your business's capacity incrementally. This approach lets you manage costs more effectively and make adjustments based on initial results before full-scale implementation.

Financial risk is another primary consideration. Expansion often requires significant investment in marketing, new staff, and possibly new locations or equipment. Careful financial planning and management are vital to ensure that you do not overextend your business financially. Regularly review your financial performance against your growth targets and adjust your strategies as necessary to ensure sustainability.

Finally, maintaining the quality of your product or service as you scale is crucial. Growth should preserve the value that made your business successful initially. Implement quality control systems and gather customer feedback continuously to ensure that your standards remain high, even as you expand. This not only helps maintain your current customer base but also enhances your reputation in new markets.

Expanding your market reach can significantly enhance your business's profitability and resilience. By carefully identifying new opportunities, scaling your operations strategically, leveraging digital marketing, and managing associated risks, you can ensure that your business not only grows but thrives in new environments. These strategies prepare you for successful expansion and ensure that your business remains adaptable and competitive in an ever-changing market landscape.

FIVE

Operations and Technology

I magine you're setting up the ultimate workspace for your startup. It needs to be efficient, adaptive, and ready to grow as you do. You wouldn't fill it with clunky, outdated equipment that doesn't communicate with each other, right? Well, the digital tools and apps you choose are the virtual equivalents of your physical workspace. They can propel your productivity or hold you back, depending on their effectiveness and integration. In this chapter, we'll sift through the digital toolbox, picking out the must-have tools that keep your operations smooth and your team in sync, all without breaking the bank.

5.1 Essential Business Tools and Apps for Startups

Overview of Tools

Navigating the sea of available business tools and apps can be overwhelming, but some categories are essential for nearly any startup. Communication tools connect your team, whether remote or in the office, ensuring that everyone is just a click away from a quick chat or a video call. Finance tools are crucial for keeping your books in order and tracking every dollar that comes in or goes out. Customer service tools help you manage customer interactions and ensure you're providing support where and when it's needed. Lastly, project management tools bring all your tasks into one visible place, helping you keep track of progress and deadlines.

For communication, tools like Microsoft Teams allow real-time messaging and file sharing, keeping everyone on the same page. For finance, QuickBooks and Sage offer comprehensive accounting solutions that grow with your business. Zendesk or Freshdesk can elevate your customer service management, providing streamlined ticketing systems and customer feedback loops. As for project management, Asana and Trello offer intuitive interfaces to manage projects with a bird's eye view of tasks and timelines.

Cost-effective Solutions

When you're just starting out budget is often tight, but that doesn't mean you have to compromise on quality. Many essential tools have free versions that, while sometimes limited, can be quite effective for a small team. Slack, for example, offers a no-cost option that is perfect for small teams looking to improve communication. Google Workspace (formerly G Suite) provides a suite of productivity tools (like Gmail, Docs, and Drive) that are free for personal use and offer affordable business plans as your needs grow.

Moreover, open-source software can be a game-changer for startups. Tools like GIMP for graphic design or LibreOffice for office productivity are entirely free and rival their commercial counterparts in functionality. The key here is to evaluate what you need from each tool and ensure the free or low-cost options meet those needs without unnecessary extras that can clutter your operations.

Integration Capabilities

As your toolbox grows, the ability of these tools to work together becomes crucial. Integrated tools can drastically reduce the time spent on manual data entry and switching between apps, enhancing efficiency and reducing errors. Many apps now offer integrations with other tools, creating a seamless flow of information. For instance, your project management software might integrate with your communication tool, alerting the team whenever a task is updated or completed.

Choosing tools that play well together—or using platforms like Zapier to create custom integrations—can automate workflows and free up your team to focus on more important tasks. When evaluating a new tool, always check for integration capabilities with your existing tools. This foresight can save you from future headaches and ensure that your digital workspace is as connected as your physical one.

Security and Reliability

Lastly, but perhaps most importantly, the security and reliability of your chosen tools are paramount. A tool is only useful if you can rely on it to be available and secure. Downtime can stall your operations, and a security breach can have devastating consequences for your business and your customers.

When assessing tools, look for those with strong security measures in place, such as end-to-end encryption, two-factor authentication, and regular security audits. Check reviews and testimonials to gauge the tool's reliability and customer service. It's also wise to have contingency plans in place—like backup solutions and alternative tools—so that you're prepared for any situation.

Remember, the proper set of tools can make an enormous difference in how smoothly and efficiently your startup operates. By choosing wisely and focusing on essential features, integration, security, and cost-effectiveness, you'll build a solid foundation that supports your business's growth and helps you navigate the exciting challenges of entrepreneurship.

In the spirit of maintaining that efficiency, let's move on to exploring effective project management techniques that can further streamline your operations and keep your team on track.

5.2 Project Management Techniques for Small Teams

Navigating through the complexities of project management in a small team can feel like trying to steer a nimble speedboat amidst changing tides. Every shift counts, and the proper methodology can either propel you forward efficiently or leave you circling in confusion. When you're picking a project management methodology, it's like choosing the right gear for your team's journey—whether it's Agile, Scrum, or Kanban—each brings its own set of rules and efficiencies, depending on your team's size, the sector you operate in, and the type of projects you handle.

Let's break it down. Agile is fantastic for teams that need flexibility and adaptability. It's designed to manage projects that evolve through collaboration among self-organizing teams and is particularly effective in environments where requirements morph regularly. For smaller teams, this can mean quicker adjustments to project scopes without the heavy bureaucratic overhead. Scrum, a subset of Agile, uses time-boxed periods known as sprints to focus on delivering specific features within a set timeframe. This can be particularly useful for small teams looking to make demonstrable progress in short, manageable bursts. Then there's Kanban, which is all about visualizing your work, limiting work in progress, and maximizing flow. In Kanban, work moves through a Kanban board, allowing teams to see the status of every piece of work at any time. This can be incredibly empowering for small teams, ensuring that everyone knows what to work on and can see how their work connects to the bigger picture.

When it comes to tools that help manage these methodologies, there are several that are tailor-made for small teams, focusing on boosting productivity without overwhelming users with complexity. Tools like Trello offer a visual approach with their card-based system that works exceptionally well with Kanban. For those utilizing Scrum, Asana provides features like task boards and timelines that help keep sprints on track. And for teams looking towards a more integrated Agile approach, Monday.com allows for flexibility with multiple project views, be it Kanban boards, timelines, or custom workflows. These tools not only help in assigning tasks and tracking progress but also foster collaboration through features like comments, attachments, and integrations with other tools.

Effective communication is the glue that holds project management together, especially in small teams where roles often overlap, and flexibility is key. Clear, consistent communication can be the difference between a project delivered smoothly and one that stumbles at every hurdle. Implementing daily stand-ups can be a game-changer here. These quick, 15-minute meetings are a staple of Agile methodologies but can be adapted for any framework. They help the team to stay updated on progress, pinpoint roadblocks, and realign on goals. Tools like Zoom or Microsoft Teams can facilitate these meetings virtually if team members are remote, ensuring no one is out of the loop regardless of their physical location.

Monitoring and evaluation are crucial in steering projects toward successful completion. This isn't just about tracking whether tasks are completed on time but also involves evaluating the quality of outcomes and the effectiveness of workflows. Setting up a dashboard using project management software can give you real-time insights into project metrics, from overall progress to individual task status. This ongoing monitoring acts as your project's compass, guiding your team through the project landscape, adjusting routes as needed to avoid roadblocks, and ensuring you remain on the path to delivery. Regular project reviews, another staple from Agile practices, can further enhance this process. These reviews provide a forum for reflective learning, allowing the team to discuss what went well, what didn't, and how processes can be improved in future cycles.

By adopting these project management techniques and tools, you can ensure that your small team not only survives but thrives in the dynamic and often turbulent waters of project execution. With the proper methodologies, tools, and communication strategies in place your team can navigate projects with precision, ensuring timely delivery and high-quality outcomes.

5.3 Implementing Effective Inventory Management

Navigating the complexities of inventory management is akin to balancing a scale meticulously; too much on one side and you risk excess; too little and you face shortages. Selecting the right inventory management system is crucial, as it forms the backbone of how you track and control your inventory. Various systems range from simple spreadsheet-based solutions to sophisticated software that integrates with other business operations like sales and purchasing. The choice largely depends on the size of your business and the complexity of your inventory needs.

For small startups a straightforward, cloud-based inventory management tool can often suffice. These systems allow you to monitor stock levels, track orders, and analyze inventory data in real time from anywhere. They're not only affordable but also scalable as your business grows. For larger operations, more robust systems like ERP (Enterprise Resource Planning) solutions might be necessary. These integrate inventory management with other facets of the business, such as customer relationship management and accounting, providing a comprehensive overview of your company's operations.

When implementing these systems, the goal is to achieve an optimal balance between supply and demand. This is where techniques like Just-In-Time (JIT) inventory management come into play. JIT involves keeping inventory levels as low as possible, ordering stock just in time for it to be used in production or sold. This approach can significantly reduce inventory costs and minimize waste, but it requires precise coordination and reliable suppliers. If you operate in a fast-paced industry where trends and customer preferences shift rapidly, JIT can give you the agility to adapt quickly without being burdened by unsold stock.

However, JIT isn't without its risks. It makes you more susceptible to supply chain disruptions. To mitigate this, you might consider a hybrid approach, where critical components are kept in stock while less crucial items are ordered as needed. This strategy provides a safety buffer while still maintaining much of the cost efficiency of JIT.

Using Data for Forecasting

In today's data-driven world, the ability to predict future inventory needs is invaluable. Historical sales data can provide insights into seasonal trends, sales cycles, and customer preferences, helping you forecast demand more accurately. By analyzing past sales patterns, you can identify when demand for certain products peaks and when it wanes, allowing you to adjust your inventory levels accordingly.

Advanced inventory management systems often include built-in analytics tools that can automate much of this analysis, providing forecasts based on various scenarios. These tools can also highlight anomalies in your data, such as sudden spikes or drops in demand that may require further investigation. For instance, if you notice an unexpected increase in sales of a particular product, it could be due to a new trend or a successful marketing campaign. By understanding the drivers behind these trends you can better prepare your inventory to meet customer demand.

Reducing Costs Through Efficient Inventory Management

Effective inventory management goes beyond just meeting customer demand; it's also about improving your bottom line. Excess inventory ties up capital that could be used elsewhere in your business, while stockouts can lead to lost sales and disgruntled customers. By maintaining optimal inventory levels you can reduce storage costs, minimize losses from unsold goods, and improve cash flow.

One way to achieve this is through regular inventory audits. These help ensure that the inventory data in your system matches the actual stock on your shelves. Discrepancies can indicate issues such as theft, damage, or data entry errors, which can lead to poor inventory decisions. Regular audits help keep your data accurate and reliable, ensuring that your inventory management system remains a valuable tool for decision-making.

Automated ordering systems can also help reduce costs by ensuring you only order what stock is necessary. These systems can be set to automatically reorder stock when levels fall below a predetermined threshold, ensuring you always have enough to meet customer demand without overstocking.

5.4 Cybersecurity Basics for Small Businesses

In today's digital age, cybersecurity is no longer a concern exclusive to giant corporations. Small businesses, with their often limited budgets for sophisticated security, are increasingly becoming tempting targets for cybercriminals. Understanding the landscape of cyber threats is crucial, as is establishing robust defenses to protect your hard-earned business assets. Let's delve into the types of cybersecurity threats that you, as a small business owner, should be particularly vigilant about.

Phishing attacks, where deceptive emails or messages trick employees into revealing sensitive information, are alarmingly common. These messages often mimic legitimate communications from trusted entities, luring the unsuspecting recipient into downloading malware or entering confidential information on a rigged website. Then there's malware, a broad term that includes viruses, worms, and ransomware—malicious software designed to disrupt, damage, or gain unauthorized access to your computer system. Ransomware deserves a special mention for its destructive potential; it encrypts your data, effectively locking you out of your systems, and demands a ransom to restore access. Data breaches, where sensitive data is accessed without authorization, can devastate your business's reputation and finances, not to mention the legal repercussions that often follow.

To combat these threats, a checklist of cybersecurity basics can serve as your first line of defense. Start with secure passwords—those that combine letters, numbers, and symbols, and are unique to each account. Encourage or, better yet, enforce a policy where employees change their passwords regularly and use multi-factor authentication for an added layer of security. Regular software updates are another non-negotiable practice. These updates patch security vulnerabilities and enhance the functionality of your software, making it harder for cybercriminals to exploit known loopholes. Anti-virus protection should be robust and up-to-date, capable of detecting and quarantining threats before they inflict damage.

The human element in cybersecurity cannot be overstated. Employee training on the best security practices forms a critical component of your cybersecurity strategy. Regular training sessions can help ingrain safe internet and email habits, such as recognizing the signs of phishing attempts and understanding the importance of not downloading unfamiliar attachments or clicking suspicious links. Clear policies should also be established outlining acceptable use of company devices, data handling procedures, and the steps to follow in the event of a suspected security breach. These policies help create a culture of security awareness and compliance among your team, making each member a vigilant custodian of your digital assets.

An often overlooked but vital aspect of cybersecurity is having an incident response plan. This plan is your playbook for dealing with security breaches—detailing steps to assess and contain the damage, notify affected parties, and recover compromised data. Start by identifying key assets and potential vulnerabilities, then outline specific response strategies for different types of security incidents. Assign roles and responsibilities, ensuring everyone knows what to do in the event of an attack. Regular drills or simulations can help fine-tune your response plan, ensuring it's robust and effective when needed.

Implementing these cybersecurity fundamentals won't just protect your business from digital threats; it will also enhance your credibility and trustworthiness in the eyes of your customers. In a world where data breaches regularly make headlines, showing that you take cybersecurity seriously can be a significant competitive advantage. Remember, the goal of cybersecurity is not just to protect technology but to safeguard your business's reputation, operational continuity, and legal compliance.

5.5 Automation and AI: Reducing Costs and Enhancing Capability

Automation and artificial intelligence (AI) are not just buzzwords; they are transformative tools that are reshaping how businesses operate, especially for small businesses looking to enhance efficiency and reduce operational costs. At its core, automation involves using technology to perform tasks that typically require human input, thereby freeing up time for you and your team to focus on more strategic activities. AI takes this a step further by not only performing tasks but also learning from them and adapting over time to increase efficiency and effectiveness.

For instance, consider the repetitive task of scheduling appointments or sending out reminder emails. Automation tools can handle these tasks effortlessly, ensuring they are completed promptly without manual intervention. AI comes into play with customer service chatbots. These tools can handle basic inquiries, learn from interactions, and gradually handle more complex queries, providing a responsive customer service experience without requiring constant human oversight.

When implementing these technologies, several accessible tools stand out, particularly for small businesses mindful of budget constraints. Platforms like Zapier offer automation across a wide range of applications, enabling you to connect different services (like Gmail, Slack, and Salesforce) to automate workflows. For AI, tools like Chatbot.com provide an affordable way to integrate basic AI chatbots into your customer service strategy. These tools are designed with non-technical users in mind, meaning you don't need a background in coding to get started.

Case Studies

Let's look at real-world applications to understand better how small businesses are leveraging automation and AI. Take, for example, a small online retail store that implemented an auto-mated inventory management system. This system tracks stock levels in real time, automatically reorders products when supplies run low, and predicts inventory needs based on sales trends. The result? The store saw a significant reduction in overstock and understock situations, leading to smoother operations and improved cash flow.

Another case involves a boutique marketing firm that used AI to enhance its customer data analysis. By implementing an AI-driven analytics tool, the firm could more accurately segment its customer base, tailor marketing campaigns to individual customer preferences, and track the effectiveness of different strategies. This targeted approach led to higher conversion rates and a better return on marketing investments.

Future Trends

Looking ahead, the future of automation and AI in small businesses is incredibly promising. One of the exciting trends on the horizon is the integration of AI with the Internet of Things (IoT). As more devices become connected, AI can help analyze the vast amounts of data these devices generate, uncovering insights that can lead to more informed business decisions. For example, a small manufacturing business might use AI to analyze data from connected machinery to predict when equipment is likely to fail and schedule maintenance proactively.

Another emerging trend is the use of AI for personalized customer experiences. AI can analyze individual customer behaviors and preferences to tailor recommendations, customize marketing messages, and even adjust pricing in real time to maximize sales potential.

The potential for AI and automation to transform small businesses is vast and continues to grow. As these technologies become more accessible and cost-effective, they offer a valuable opportunity for small business owners to improve efficiency, reduce costs, and stay competitive in a rapidly evolving market.

SIX

Managing Risks and Legal Compliance

I magine setting sail on the vast ocean in your very own ship— the entrepreneurial vessel. Just as a seasoned captain navigates through storms and avoids hidden reefs, you too must steer your business through the rough waters of risks and legal challenges. But fear not, for every captain has a map and a compass, and in this chapter, I'll equip you with your very own: a thorough understanding of risk management tailored for startups like yours.

6.1 Risk Assessment for Startups: Identifying Potential Threats

Navigating the seas of business isn't just about keeping your eyes on the distant horizon; it's also about being aware of the immediate dangers that lurk beneath the waters. These dangers, or risks, come in various forms—operational, financial, strategic, and compliance. Operational risks could be anything from a breakdown in your production line to a failure in your supply chain that delays delivery times. Financial risks might involve unexpected costs eating into your margins or a client that suddenly cancels a lucrative contract. Strategic risks are about the decisions you make regarding the direction of your business. What if the market doesn't react to your new product launch the way you anticipated? Lastly, compliance risks include failing to adhere to laws and regulations, which can lead to fines and damage to your reputation.

Conducting a risk assessment might sound as daunting as charting a course through a hurricane, but it can be broken down into manageable steps. First, you need to identify your assets—what's at stake? This includes physical assets like your inventory and equipment, as well as intangibles like your brand reputation and customer trust. Next, evaluate the threats each of these assets faces. This involves thinking about scenarios that could lead to harm. For instance, what would happen if a key supplier went out of business? How would you handle a data breach involving sensitive customer information?

Once you've mapped out the potential threats, it's time to estimate their impact. This isn't just about considering the worst-case scenario; it's about understanding the range of possible outcomes and how likely they are to occur. This will help you prioritize which risks need immediate attention and which could be more of a long-term concern.

Now, you're ready to develop risk mitigation strategies. These are your action plans for reducing the likelihood of risks occurring or minimizing their impact if they do. Prevention plans may include installing security systems to protect against theft or training employees on compliance standards to avoid legal issues. Contingency measures could involve setting up emergency funds or having backup suppliers in place. And when certain risks can't be avoided or absorbed internally, risk transfer options such as purchasing insurance come into play.

Interactive Element: Risk Assessment Worksheet

To help you apply these concepts I've included a Risk Assessment Worksheet. This tool will guide you through the process of identifying, evaluating, and prioritizing risks. By filling out this worksheet, you'll develop a clearer picture of the potential challenges your startup might face and start crafting strategies to navigate these waters safely.

By the end of this exercise, you'll have not just a list of potential threats but a robust strategy to address them, ensuring that your entrepreneurial journey isn't derailed by the unexpected.

6.2 Legal Pitfalls and How to Avoid Them: A Legal Advisor's Tips

Navigating the legal landscape of business ownership is akin to walking through a minefield; one wrong step can have significant repercussions. Common legal mistakes often trip up new entrepreneurs, and being aware of these can save you not only headaches but potentially substantial financial costs. For instance, many startups falter by not adhering to licensing laws, a fundamental aspect of legal compliance that varies widely depending on the industry and location of your business. Whether it's a city business license, a health department permit for a restaurant, or a professional license for a real estate agency, ensuring you have the proper permits and licenses before you start operating is crucial.

Another frequent misstep involves the misclassification of employees. In the zeal to cut costs, startups might wrongly classify workers as independent contractors rather than employees. This can lead to severe penalties, back taxes, and damaged relationships with workers. It's vital to understand the legal definitions and criteria for each classification, as dictated by the IRS and the Department of Labor. Similarly, copyright laws are often overlooked in the digital age, where content can be easily downloaded and shared. However, using copyrighted materials without permission can lead to lawsuits and hefty fines. Always ensure you have the right to use or reproduce any materials not created by your company, and consider protecting your original content with copyright registration.

Now, let's talk about zoning laws, which can be particularly nuanced and often catch many entrepreneurs off guard. Zoning regulations govern how a property can be used and can vary dramatically from one area to another. For instance, operating a manufacturing business in an area zoned for residential use is typically a violation. To ensure compliance, you should start by consulting your local planning agency to understand the specific regulations applicable to your intended business location. They can provide guidance on zoning restrictions, and if necessary, you might need to apply for a variance or conditional-use permit. This proactive approach not only avoids legal issues but also cements the legitimacy and stability of your business operations.

Thorough and accurate documentation is your safety net in the legal world. It proves compliance, supports claims, and clarifies agreements. Start by keeping detailed records of all business transactions, contracts, employee interactions, and regulatory compliance efforts. This documentation will be invaluable during audits, legal disputes, or sale negotiations. It acts as both a shield and as evidence, providing clear proof of your business's operations and adherence to laws. Implement a regular schedule for reviewing and updating documentation, ensuring all business activities are accurately reflected and stored securely. Digital tools and cloud storage can offer efficient ways to manage and safeguard your documents.

Lastly, the complexity of legal matters often necessitates professional advice. Knowing when and why to seek legal advice can be the difference between a minor issue and a catastrophic legal entanglement. Routine matters such as contract reviews, trademark registrations, or employee handbooks might be well-served by legal templates or more cost-effective legal service platforms. However, for more complex issues like mergers, acquisitions, or serious legal disputes, hiring a qualified attorney is advisable. When choosing an attorney, look for someone with expertise relevant to your industry and a track record of working with similar-sized businesses. A good lawyer will not only guide you through complex legal landscapes but also help preempt potential legal issues before they arise, acting as a true partner in your business's growth and longevity. Remember, investing in competent legal advice is not an expense; it's a safeguard for your business's future.

6.3 Data Protection and Privacy Laws: What You Need to Know

In today's digital age, protecting the personal data of your customers isn't just a good practice—it's a legal requirement that can significantly impact your business's credibility and bottom line. As you navigate the complexities of data protection laws, you must be well-versed in regulations like the General Data Protection Regulation (GDPR) in the EU, the California Consumer Privacy Act (CCPA) in the U.S., and other local laws that might affect your operations. These laws are designed to protect consumer rights and ensure businesses handle personal data responsibly.

The GDPR, for example, has set a new benchmark globally for privacy laws, emphasizing transparency, accountability, and consumer rights. It applies to any business, regardless of location, that processes the personal data of EU citizens. Key provisions include the requirement for clear consent to process data, the right for individuals to access their personal data, and strict guidelines on data breach notifications. Similarly, the CCPA provides California residents with the right to know about the personal data collected on them, the purpose of collection, and to whom it is being sold or disclosed.

To comply with these laws, you must understand the specific rights they grant to data subjects. These include, but are not limited to, the right to access their data, the right to request deletion of their data, and the right to opt out of data selling. Implementing procedures to respond to these rights requests within the stipulated time frames is essential. Additionally, conducting Data Protection Impact Assessments (DPIAs) for processing activities that pose a high risk to individuals' rights and freedoms becomes crucial. DPIAs help identify and minimize the data protection risks of a project and are a proactive way of demonstrating compliance and accountability.

Practical Measures for Data Protection

When it comes to safeguarding personal data, several practical measures can be implemented to ensure robust protection. Encryption is a fundamental technique where data is encoded so only authorized parties can access it. Whether data is at rest on your servers or in transit via the internet, encryption acts as a critical barrier against unauthorized access. Secure data storage solutions are equally important. Opt for storage options that offer built-in security features such as automatic backups, data redundancy, and secure access controls.

Another vital strategy is adopting a privacy-by-design approach. This means integrating data protection principles right from the technological design phase and throughout the lifecycle of the product or service. This approach not only helps in complying with privacy laws but also builds trust with your customers, showing that their data is considered and protected from the outset.

Handling Data Breaches

Despite your best efforts data breaches can still occur, and how you handle them can significantly affect your business's reputation and compliance. The first step is to have an incident response plan in place. This plan should outline the immediate actions to take once a breach is detected, such as containing the breach, assessing the risks associated with the breached data, and notifying the relevant authorities and affected parties. For instance, under the GDPR, businesses must report certain types of data breaches to the appropriate data protection authority within 72 hours of becoming aware of the breach, unless the breach is unlikely to result in a risk to the rights and freedoms of individuals.

Informing affected individuals is also crucial, especially if the breach could result in discrimination, damage to reputation, financial loss, or other significant economic or social disadvantages. Transparency in your communications about what occurred, the potential impacts, and how you are addressing it helps maintain trust and may mitigate the damage to your business.

Finally, analyzing the breach and learning from it is essential to prevent future incidents. Review and update your security measures and response plans regularly to address any identified weaknesses. Training employees in data protection best practices and breach response can also significantly reduce the risk of future breaches by ensuring they understand the importance of safeguarding data and the procedures to follow in the event of a breach.

Navigating data protection and privacy laws can seem daunting. Still, with a clear understanding of the regulations, practical security measures in place, and a solid response plan, you can ensure your business not only complies with the laws but also respects and protects the personal data of your customers, thereby enhancing your business's integrity and trustworthiness.

6.4 Employee Laws and Regulations: Hiring and Management Compliance

Navigating the waters of employment law is akin to setting up the rules of engagement for your team, ensuring that every member can contribute to your venture in a safe, fair, and regulated environment. As you build your team, you'll encounter laws designed to protect both you and your employees. These range from anti-discrimination statutes that ensure a fair hiring process to wage and hour laws that govern compensation, not to mention regulations regarding employee benefits, which cover everything from health insurance to retirement plans.

Let's start by unpacking the legal framework that surrounds hiring. First off, anti-discrimination laws are pivotal. Under laws like the Equal Employment Opportunity (EEO) regulations, it's illegal to make employment decisions based on factors such as race, color, religion, sex, or national origin. This extends to your job advertisements, interview questions, and any employment tests you might administer. For instance, asking a candidate about their marital status or whether they plan to have children can be considered discriminatory and could land your business in hot water. Instead, focus on questions that directly relate to the candidate's ability to perform the job duties.

Background checks can be a valuable tool in your hiring arsenal, helping you make informed decisions about potential hires. However, compliance with the Fair Credit Reporting Act (FCRA) is crucial here. You must obtain the candidate's written consent before conducting any background check, and if the information you discover forms the basis for a decision not to hire, you must provide the candidate with a copy of the report and a summary of their rights under the FCRA before you take any final action. This ensures transparency and gives the candidate a fair chance to contest any inaccuracies.

Drafting employment agreements is another critical step. These documents should clearly outline the terms of employment, including job duties, compensation, and termination conditions. It's essential to ensure these agreements comply with local and federal laws. For instance, if you include a non-compete clause, it must be reasonable in terms of time, geographical scope, and the type of work restricted. Courts can deem Overly restrictive non-compete clauses unenforceable, which could leave your business vulnerable.

Maintaining a compliant workplace is an ongoing process that extends beyond hiring. This involves creating a work environment that adheres to safety regulations, handling employee grievances appropriately, and managing employment records diligently. For instance, the Occupational Safety and Health Administration (OSHA) sets out specific guidelines for workplace safety that include everything from required signage to emergency exits and proper handling of hazardous materials. Compliance isn't just about avoiding fines—it's about creating a workplace where employees feel safe and valued.

Handling employee grievances is another area where legal compliance plays a crucial role. Establishing a straightforward, fair process for addressing employee concerns not only helps in resolving issues efficiently but also protects your business from potential lawsuits. This process should be documented in your employee handbook and should detail how employees can file a complaint, the steps you will take to investigate it, and how a resolution will be reached. Ensuring that this process is followed consistently can help maintain morale and trust among your team.

Navigating employee terminations requires a careful approach to comply with employment laws and to protect your business from potential legal challenges. Whether an employee is being let go due to performance issues, redundancy, or misconduct, it's crucial to handle the termination process sensitively and legally. Documentation is your best defense here. Keeping detailed records of employment issues, performance reviews, and disciplinary actions can support your decision if the termination is ever challenged in court.

Severance agreements can be useful tools in ensuring a smooth parting of ways. They offer benefits to the departing employee in exchange for waiving certain legal claims against the company. However, for these agreements to be enforceable, they must be drafted correctly and offer something of value to which the employee is not already entitled. For example, additional compensation or benefits should be provided in exchange for the employee's agreement not to sue for wrongful termination.

In conclusion, embedding a deep understanding and respect for employment laws into your business operations is not merely about legal compliance—it's about fostering a professional, respectful, and equitable workplace.

6.5 Creating Contracts: A Guide for Entrepreneurs

Stepping into the realm of business contracts can feel like navigating a dense forest – you need a clear path to ensure you don't lose your way. Let's break down the essentials of what makes a contract not only valid but also robust enough to protect your interests. Every solid contract starts with four fundamental elements: offer, acceptance, consideration, and mutual consent. An offer is what one party proposes to do, for example, deliver a service or supply goods. Acceptance must then be clear and unambiguous, reflecting a mirror image of the offer without any deviations, which could otherwise be seen as a counteroffer. Consideration refers to what is exchanged between the parties involved—this could be money, services, or even an agreement to refrain from a particular action. Finally, mutual consent implies that both parties understand and agree to the contract's terms, free from any form of duress or undue influence.

Diving deeper, startups especially need to familiarize themselves with various types of contracts that are particularly relevant to their operations. Partnership agreements lay the foundation for any business partnership, detailing each partner's responsibilities, profit share, and decision-making powers. Service contracts are crucial when you hire third parties to perform services for your business; these should outline the scope of work, deadlines, payment terms, and confidentiality clauses. Non-disclosure agreements (NDAs), on the other hand, are essential for protecting sensitive information, especially when you're sharing business ideas or data with potential partners or employees.

When drafting a contract, clarity and thoroughness are your best tools. Start by clearly defining the terms and conditions of the agreement, avoiding any legal jargon that might obscure the meaning. Be explicit about every obligation and right that each party holds. For instance, if you're drafting a service contract, specify the exact nature of the services to be provided, when and how they are to be delivered, and the precise amount and payment terms. Including a detailed clause about what happens if either party fails to meet their obligations can save you from potential disputes. It's also wise to include a termination clause that outlines how either party can end the contract if things don't go as planned.

Negotiating a contract is much like a dance. It requires patience, keen observation, and an understanding of when to lead and when to follow. Begin negotiations with a clear understanding of your non-negotiables—those terms that you cannot compromise on. However, also identify areas where you are willing to be flexible. Effective negotiation is not about defeating the other party but finding a win-win solution that benefits both sides. Strategies such as 'bundling' concessions—combining several small concessions into one request—can often be more palatable to the other party and lead to better outcomes. Always approach negotiations with a cooperative attitude; remember, the goal is to build a relationship that could contribute to your business's success in the long run.

Contracts are more than just paperwork; they are a foundational element of your business's legal and operational framework. They ensure that each party knows exactly what is expected, providing a roadmap that can help navigate the complexities of business relationships. By understanding the essentials of contract law, mastering the art of contract drafting, and honing your negotiation skills, you can set your business up for success in any venture you undertake.

6.6 Business Continuity Planning: Preparing for the Unexpected

Imagine this: a major storm knocks out your primary supplier's warehouse, or a sudden cyberattack locks you out of your customer data. Such scenarios can seriously affect unprepared businesses. That's where a solid business continuity plan (BCP) comes into play, acting as a life jacket that keeps your business afloat during disasters and unforeseen events. The importance of having a BCP cannot be overstated—it ensures that your operations can continue with minimal disruption, safeguarding your assets, reputation, and the overall health of your enterprise.

A comprehensive BCP begins with a thorough risk assessment, much like the ones we discussed earlier, but with a focus tailored specifically to business disruptions. Next comes a business impact analysis (BIA), which pinpoints the functions critical for your business's survival and estimates the impact of their disruption. The BIA helps you understand which areas of your business to prioritize in recovery efforts, ensuring that resources are allocated efficiently in a crisis.

Next, recovery strategies form the core of your BCP. These strategies should outline specific steps to recover critical functions and systems. For instance, if an online retailer loses its e-commerce platform, a recovery strategy might involve switching to a temporary manual order processing system while the primary system is restored. Other strategies may include setting up reciprocal agreements with other businesses for shared use of facilities and resources, or contracting with vendors for priority service in emergencies.

Regular testing and updating of your BCP are crucial. Just as sailors regularly check and adjust their equipment to prepare for changing sea conditions, you should periodically test your BCP through drills and simulations. These tests can reveal weaknesses in your plan and provide insights that help you make necessary adjustments. Additionally, your BCP should be a living document that evolves as your business grows and changes. Regular reviews —a minimum of once a year or after any significant business change—ensure that your plan always aligns with your current business structure and needs.

Leveraging Technology for Continuity

In today's tech-driven world, several technological solutions can bolster your business continuity efforts. Cloud storage, for example, plays a pivotal role in data protection. By storing data off-site in the cloud, you ensure it remains accessible and safe from local disasters. In the event of data loss on local servers, you can quickly restore data from the cloud, minimizing downtime and data corruption risks.

Remote work solutions have also proven invaluable, such as those observed during global events like the COVID-19 pandemic. Tools that support telecommuting—such as virtual private networks (VPNs), video conferencing, and collaborative online workspaces —can keep your team working effectively, even if they can't access your physical business premises.

Automated backups are another critical technology strategy. Setting up automated systems to back up your data regularly— ideally in real-time or at least daily—ensures that you always have a recent copy of your data from which to restore should the need arise. Automation removes the risk of human error and ensures backups are performed consistently without fail.

Implementing these technologies not only supports your business continuity planning but also enhances your everyday operational efficiency and resilience against minor disruptions. By integrating these tech solutions into your BCP, you equip your business with the tools to not only survive but thrive in the face of adversity.

The risk landscape is as varied as it is unpredictable. By preparing for the unexpected with a robust business continuity plan, understanding the legal nuances of running a startup, protecting your data, and ensuring compliance in all aspects of operations, you set a solid foundation for your business's success and longevity.

SEVEN

Human Resources and Team Building

Think of building your team like assembling a top-tier sports squad: every player has a specific role that's crucial to the team's overall success, and finding the right fit for each position is instrumental to winning the game. In the bustling arena of small business, where every team member's contribution can have a significant impact, perfecting your recruiting strategies becomes not just important but essential to your business's success story. This section dives into the nuts and bolts of recruiting—the art and science of attracting, evaluating, and securing the right talent to grow your business.

7.1 Recruiting Strategies for Small Businesses: Finding the Right Fit

Defining Job Requirements

Imagine you're drafting the blueprint for the ideal candidate. This isn't just about listing desired qualifications and skills; it's about aligning these with your company's goals and the specific demands of the position. Start by conducting a thorough job analysis which involves examining the tasks, responsibilities, and outcomes associated with the role. Engage with stakeholders, including those currently in the role or those directly interacting with it, to gain insights into the day-to-day activities and long-term expectations. This deep dive helps you craft a job description that goes beyond the basics—incorporating elements of your company culture and the personal attributes that thrive within it. Clarity here ensures that candidates understand not just the "what" of the job but the "why" and the "how," making it easier to attract those who resonate with your mission and work style.

Effective Recruitment Channels

Casting a wide net might seem like a good strategy, but when resources are limited, precision matters. Each recruitment channel has its strengths, and selecting the right mix can dramatically enhance your recruitment efforts. Online job portals like Indeed and Glassdoor are great for a broad reach, but don't overlook the power of social media platforms like LinkedIn, which allows for a more targeted approach and the opportunity to engage directly with potential candidates. Industry-specific forums and professional networks can also be gold mines for niche skills and are often frequented by candidates who are passionate about their specialties. Additionally, never underestimate the value of networking events; they provide a personal touch to recruitment, offering real-time interaction and the chance to see candidates in a more dynamic setting. Combining these channels ensures a diversified approach to attracting talent, enhancing your chances of finding the right fit for your team.

Interview Techniques

Interviewing is where the rubber meets the road. It's your opportunity to see beyond the resume and assess whether a candidate is indeed the right fit for your team. Incorporate a mix of behavioral-based questions and task-oriented assessments to get a comprehensive view of the candidate's capabilities and work style. Behavioral questions like, "Can you describe a situation where you had to overcome a significant challenge at work?" help you understand how a candidate operates under pressure and adapts to complex situations. Complement these with practical assessments relevant to the job. For instance, if you're hiring a graphic designer, a short design test could reveal more about their actual skills than hours of conversation. Remember, the goal of the interview is not just to validate skills but to sense the candidate's alignment with your company's culture and values.

Leveraging Technology in Recruitment

In the digital age, recruitment technology can provide a significant advantage. Applicant Tracking Systems (ATS) are invaluable for managing applications efficiently, helping you track and filter candidates based on predefined criteria. More advanced AI-driven tools can further streamline the recruitment process, from automating initial candidate screenings based on keyword matching to deploying chatbots that engage with candidates in preliminary discussions. These technologies not only save time but also enhance the candidate experience, portraying your company as modern and tech-savvy. However, while these tools aid in efficiency, they should complement—not replace—the human element of hiring, which is crucial for assessing the nuanced aspects of a candidate's fit.

By mastering these aspects of recruiting, you set the stage not just to fill a position but to enhance your team's dynamics and drive your business forward. Remember, each new hire is not just an addition to your workforce but a potential catalyst for innovation and growth, making effective recruiting a cornerstone of your business strategy.

7.2 Onboarding New Employees: Creating a Smooth Transition

Imagine you've just recruited a fantastic new team member, and now it's time to integrate them into your company. Think of onboarding not just as a routine checklist of tasks to complete but as a critical phase that sets the tone for an employee's experience at your company. A well-structured onboarding program does more than introduce your new hire to the nuts and bolts of the job; it immerses them in your company culture, primes them for success, and builds a foundational connection that can boost long-term retention.

The onboarding process should begin the moment a candidate accepts your offer. Start with administrative setup, which covers the essentials like employment paperwork, setting up email accounts, and providing necessary hardware. This phase is crucial and must be handled efficiently to avoid costly delays that can dampen a new hire's enthusiasm. Next, focus on a comprehensive training program tailored to their role. This isn't just about job duties; it's about understanding the company's strategic goals, how their role contributes to these objectives, and how they can navigate its processes and systems. Include sessions on the tools they'll use daily, whether it's project management software, sales databases, or design platforms, ensuring they feel equipped and empowered.

Initial assignments should be carefully chosen to provide mean-ingful, attainable goals. Start with smaller projects that contribute to larger tasks or team objectives. This approach helps new hires build confidence and demonstrate their immediate impact. Remember, the goal of these early assignments is not only to assess their skills but also to integrate them into the team, fostering connections and collaboration.

Assigning mentors is like giving your new hire a personal guide to the company. A good mentor does more than answer questions; they help new employees navigate the company culture, introduce them to key teammates, and provide insights into how to succeed within the organization. This relationship can significantly speed up the integration of new hires because it creates a more personal-ized and supportive entry into the company. Choose mentors who are not only knowledgeable but also embody the company's values and have a genuine interest in helping others grow.

Gathering feedback during the onboarding process is essential, and it's a two-way street. Regular check-ins, where new hires can share their experiences and voice any concerns, help you gauge the effectiveness of your onboarding process. Use this feedback to make immediate adjustments, such as clarifying misunderstand-ings or providing additional resources. Over time, this feedback can inform broader improvements to the onboarding program, ensuring it remains responsive to the needs of future hires.

Setting clear expectations and goals from the outset is crucial. This clarity helps eliminate confusion and aligns the new employee's efforts with the company's objectives. During the first few weeks, sit down with your new hire to outline what success looks like in their role. Discuss short-term goals for the onboarding period and longer-term expectations for their first year. This meeting should be a dialogue, giving the new hire the opportunity to ask questions and express their perceptions of their role and contributions.

This proactive approach to onboarding new employees sets them up for success, enhances team dynamics, and bolsters overall company performance. By investing in a thorough onboarding process, you're not just filling a vacancy; you're enriching your team's culture and capability, paving the way for sustained growth and innovation in your business.

7.3 Leadership Skills for New Entrepreneurs: Inspiring Your Team

Fundamental Leadership Qualities

Stepping into the shoes of a leader, especially as a new entrepreneur, means more than just managing tasks and timelines —it's about embodying qualities that inspire and drive your team toward success. Integrity, adaptability, and vision stand out as cornerstone qualities for effective leadership. Integrity involves consistently aligning your actions with your values and creating a trustful and ethical environment. For you, this might mean being transparent about business challenges or making sure your dealings are always above board, which in turn fosters trust and respect among your team members.

Adaptability is particularly crucial in the dynamic landscape of a startup. It's the ability to pivot strategies, embrace new ideas, or change course in response to feedback or changing market conditions. You can cultivate this by staying open to learning and being willing to admit when a different approach may be necessary. This openness not only helps you navigate the business terrain with agility but also sets a powerful example for your team.

Vision is about having a clear, compelling idea of what you want to achieve and being able to communicate this to your team effectively. It's what rallies your team around a common goal and provides a sense of purpose. Developing a clear vision involves:

- Deep reflection on the core purpose of your business.
- Understanding where you want it to go.
- Imagining the impact you want it to have on the world.

Sharing this vision with your team helps them see where they fit into the bigger picture and why their contributions matter.

Your vision is the vision of your company. Your employees look up to you to guide the company and make necessary changes to continue to succeed. By adapting to the challenges that you face and moving your company forward you will instill confidence in your leadership both inside and outside.

Effective Communication Skills

In the world of startups, where every team member's role can significantly impact the outcome, effective communication becomes the lifeblood of the organization. This means not just talking but ensuring your message is clearly understood and that you're listening to feedback and ideas from the team. Regular team meetings are a good practice, where updates on progress, challenges, and strategies are shared. Equally important are one-on-one check-ins, which can help you understand individual team members' perspectives and provide a platform for them to share thoughts they might not voice in a group setting.

Transparency in your communication builds trust and ensures everyone is on the same page. For instance, sharing the reasoning behind significant decisions or changes in strategy can help alleviate uncertainties and foster a sense of inclusion and respect. Additionally, make sure to communicate in a way that aligns with your team's diverse preferences—some might prefer detailed emails, others brief face-to-face conversations, and still others might benefit from visual data presentations.

Motivation and Team Building

Creating an environment where team members are motivated and engaged often leads to higher productivity and better results. Recognizing achievements, whether through a simple thank-you in a meeting or more formal rewards helps individuals feel valued for their contributions. Setting goals that are challenging yet achievable is also crucial. These goals should stretch your team's abilities but also be attainable, which can enhance motivation and the satisfaction that comes from achieving them.

Fostering a collaborative environment is another critical element. Encourage team members to share ideas, work together on solutions, and support each other's professional growth. Regular brainstorming sessions or team-building exercises can enhance cohesion and encourage a more collaborative culture. Remember, a motivated team is not just about pushing toward business goals but also about building a community that supports and enriches its members.

Dealing with Underperformance

Addressing underperformance is a delicate aspect of leadership that requires a thoughtful and constructive approach. Start by ensuring that performance expectations are made clear from the outset. If underperformance is observed a private, respectful conversation to understand the root causes is essential. It could be due to unclear instructions, personal issues, or a lack of resources to complete the job effectively.

Once you understand the issue, you can work together to create a plan for improvement. This might include additional training, more regular feedback, or adjustments in workload or responsibilities. In situations where little or no progress is observed despite support and resources, reassignment or termination might be necessary as a last resort. It's critical to handle such situations carefully, ensuring that decisions are fair, documented, and communicated clearly to the individual involved.

7.4 Developing Company: Core Values and Employee Engagement

When you think about the backbone of your company, what comes to mind? It's not just your products or services but the core values that define your company's heart and soul. These are more than just words on a website; they are the guiding principles that dictate every decision and action within your organization. Defining these core values isn't about picking what sounds good; it's about digging deep to uncover what truly drives your business and aligns with your vision. To start, gather your key team members for a brainstorming session. Discuss what beliefs and principles are non-negotiable in the way you conduct business. These may include a commitment to quality, innovation, integrity, or customer satisfaction. Once defined, these core values should be communicated clearly and consistently across all levels of the company, from top executives to new hires, ensuring everyone understands and aligns with these fundamental beliefs.

But how do these core values influence day-to-day operations and behaviors? It's one thing to state that your company values' integrity,' but another to integrate it into everyday practices. For instance, if integrity is a core value, your business practices should be transparent, and ethical dilemmas should be handled openly and fairly. Embedding these values into your company's operations can involve training programs that illustrate these values in action, performance review systems that reward value-aligned behaviors, and leadership that consistently models these values.

Creating a positive work environment goes hand-in-hand with defining core values. This environment should be where employees feel valued, respected, and integral to the company's success. Flexible work policies can play a significant role here, particularly in today's dynamic work climate. Whether it's flexible hours, the option to work remotely, or compressed work weeks, these policies can help employees balance work with personal responsibilities, leading to greater job satisfaction and retention. Moreover, fostering a culture that encourages team bonding through regular team lunches, off-site team-building retreats, or collaborative projects can strengthen relationships and improve teamwork. Open communication channels are also vital; they ensure that employees feel heard and involved in the company's operations. Regular open-door policy days or scheduled 'Ask Me Anything' sessions with leadership can demystify the company's direction and decisions, making the workplace more inclusive.

Employee engagement is another critical aspect of company culture, directly influencing productivity and employee retention. Regular employee surveys can provide insights into how employees feel about their roles, the work environment, and the company's direction. These surveys should be anonymous to encourage honest feedback and conducted regularly to track changes and improvements over time. Town hall meetings, where employees can discuss recent survey results and provide additional input, can help address concerns and gather fresh ideas, enhancing engagement across the board. Additionally, providing opportunities for career development—such as workshops, training sessions, and clear pathways for advancement—can motivate employees to grow with the company, reducing turnover and fostering a workforce that is skilled and committed.

The impact of a strong company culture on performance cannot be overstated. A culture that aligns with your company's core values and provides a supportive, engaging work environment can significantly enhance employee performance. Teams in such environments tend to have higher job satisfaction, lower turnover rates, and better overall performance. Moreover, a positive company culture can be a powerful tool in attracting and retaining top talent. In today's competitive job market, a company known for its strong culture and employee satisfaction can stand out from the crowd, attracting individuals who have the skills and the desire to contribute to a vibrant and dynamic work environment.

By embracing these strategies, you can craft a company culture that reflects your core values and actively contributes to your business's success.

7.5 Handling Conflict: Resolution Strategies for Small Teams

When running a small business think of your team as a tightly knit crew on a sailboat. Smooth sailing depends on everyone working harmoniously, but even the best crews can face rough seas in the form of conflicts. Recognizing and addressing these conflicts at an early stage can prevent them from escalating and affecting your team's performance and morale. Common sources of conflict in small teams often stem from role ambiguity, resource allocation, and personality clashes. Role ambiguity occurs when team members need clarification about their responsibilities, leading to overlaps or gaps that cause friction. For instance, if two team members assume they're both leading a project, confusion and conflict might arise. Resource allocation conflicts can happen when team members feel resources like time, money, or materials aren't distributed fairly, potentially leaving some feeling undervalued or overstretched. Personality clashes are perhaps the most straightforward but also the most challenging conflicts to resolve, as they stem from fundamental differences in values, communication styles, or work habits.

It's crucial to get ahead of these issues and keep a pulse on team dynamics. Encourage an environment where feedback is shared openly and regularly. This can be facilitated through regular team meetings or anonymous surveys where team members can express concerns before they turn into larger issues. Also, setting clear roles and responsibilities right from the start, and revising them as your team grows or changes, helps minimize misunderstandings. Having a predefined process for handling conflicts when they arise shows your team that you're committed to a fair and constructive resolution.

Conflict resolution techniques are essential tools in your managerial toolkit, allowing you to smooth over issues while maintaining team cohesion. Mediation, active listening, and structured problem-solving sessions are particularly effective. Mediation involves acting as a neutral facilitator to help disputing parties understand each other's perspectives and work towards a resolution. This doesn't mean making decisions for them but guiding the conversation in a way that leads to an understanding or compromise. Active listening is another critical skill during these discussions. It involves fully concentrating on what is being said rather than passively hearing the speaker's message. This technique helps validate team members' feelings and concerns and demonstrates that you value their input, and are invested in resolving the conflict.

When structured effectively, problem-solving sessions can turn conflict into a collaborative effort to improve processes or relationships. Begin these sessions by clearly defining the problem without assigning blame. Then, encourage all parties to contribute to generating solutions, ensuring that each voice is heard and considered. This not only helps in finding a solution that is acceptable to all but also strengthens the team by involving members in the decision-making process. Throughout these processes, maintaining professionalism and respect is crucial. Doing so sets the tone for interactions and shows that while disagreements might arise, how they are handled can either positively or negatively impact the team culture.

Preventive measures are equally important and often more effective than addressing conflicts after they've escalated. Clear communication is your first line of defense. Regularly updating your team on company goals, individual roles, and project expectations helps align everyone's efforts and reduce misunderstandings. Role clarity, achieved through detailed job descriptions and regular reviews of roles, ensures that everyone knows what is expected of them and how they fit into the larger team. Regular team-building exercises can also play a significant role in preventing conflicts. By fostering an atmosphere of cooperation and understanding, these activities can help mitigate the effects of personality clashes by allowing team members to connect on a personal level, beyond their professional roles.

Conflicts aren't just challenges; they're opportunities for growth and improvement. Each conflict provides a unique window into underlying issues that, once addressed, can strengthen your team and improve your operational efficiency. After resolving a conflict, take a step back to analyze why it occurred and how it was handled. Discuss with your team what lessons can be learned and how similar situations can be avoided or better managed in the future. This learning approach not only helps in improving your conflict resolution framework but also builds a resilient team that is better equipped to handle future challenges.

By understanding the roots of conflicts and equipping yourself with effective resolution strategies, you can ensure that your team navigates these challenges successfully and emerges stronger. Remember, the goal isn't just to put out fires—it's to build a team that can withstand the heat and thrive.

7.6 Planning for Growth: When to Hire and How to Manage Expansion

Growing your business is like planting a garden; it requires careful planning, nurturing, and the right conditions to flourish. As your business expands, knowing when to add to your team is crucial. The first step in this process is assessing your hiring needs, which involves a thorough analysis of your current workforce and future business objectives. Start by identifying any skill gaps that may exist within your team. These are roles or competencies that are either insufficiently covered or completely missing but necessary for your business's growth. For example, if you're expanding your digital marketing efforts, you might need someone with expertise in SEO or social media marketing.

Evaluating the current workload of your team is equally important. Are there employees who are consistently overburdened? This not only affects their productivity and job satisfaction but could lead to burnout. Regularly review workload distributions and talk to your team about their day-to-day challenges. This will help you decide whether to hire more staff or redistribute tasks more evenly.

Forecasting future business needs involves looking ahead. Where do you see your business in the next year to five years? What roles will you need to achieve these future goals? This might involve strategic hires who can open new revenue streams or enhance innovation. For instance, hiring a business development manager could help forge new partnerships and expand into new markets.

Once you've identified the need for new hires, consider scalable hiring strategies. Developing a talent pipeline is a proactive approach that involves continuously attracting and engaging potential candidates, even before a specific role opens up. This can significantly shorten the hiring process when a position becomes available. Utilize professional networking sites like LinkedIn or industry-specific platforms to connect with potential candidates, share insights about your company's culture and projects, and keep them engaged with regular updates.

Utilizing part-time positions or freelancers can offer flexibility and cost efficiency, especially when you need specific skills for short-term projects. This approach allows you to scale your work-force up or down as needed without committing to full-time salaries and benefits. It's also a great way to evaluate a freelancer's fit with your company before offering a full-time position.

Creating scalable roles means designing jobs that can evolve as your company grows. These roles should have clear pathways for advancement and development, encouraging employees to grow with the company. For example, a junior developer might become a lead developer or even a technology director as you move forward.

Integrating new team members as your business scales involves ensuring they align well with the existing team and company culture. This alignment is crucial for maintaining a cohesive work environment. Start with a structured onboarding process that covers the practical aspects of the job and immerses new hires in your company culture. Encourage existing employees to be part of the onboarding and training process, which can foster team spirit and help new hires feel welcome.

Another challenge is maintaining your company culture and quality standards during rapid growth. It's easy for these to become lost or diminished if not consciously upheld. Involve your leadership team in defining and reinforcing the core values of your company. Regular training sessions and workshops can instill these values in new hires and remind longer-standing employees of their importance. Also, establish clear quality standards for all work outputs and ensure these are communicated and understood by all team members.

Continuous training plays a pivotal role in maintaining quality standards. As your business grows and evolves, your team's skills should grow also. Invest in training programs that not only enhance job performance but also personal development. This will boost employee morale and ensure your team can meet the challenges of a growing business.

In summary, expanding your team thoughtfully and strategically is critical to the effective management of your business's growth. You can sustain your company culture and maintain quality standards by assessing hiring needs accurately, employing scalable hiring strategies, and ensuring new team members integrate well. As you move forward, keep these strategies in mind to support your business as it scales to new heights.

Conclusion

We've journeyed together from the spark of a business idea to the nuts and bolts of running a thriving venture. We've covered the essentials—laying your foundation with the proper business structure, navigating the waters of financing, crafting a brand that stands out in the crowded marketplace, deploying effective sales strategies, and fine-tuning your operations and technologies.

Remember, the core of this adventure is about embracing change and being prepared. That means diving deep into planning, understanding your legal and financial duties, and always upholding the power of innovation and continuous learning. These elements aren't just nice-to-haves; they will keep your business dynamic, relevant, and ahead of the curve.

This book was written for you. It's here to demystify the process of launching and nurturing your business, specifically tailored to those who have yet to step into the business arena. It's designed to guide and equip you with the knowledge and tools you need to transform your business idea into a living, breathing, and successful reality.

Now, it's time for action. Take that bold step toward entrepreneurship with confidence. Remember, resilience, adaptability, and a commitment to continuous improvement are your best friends on this journey. Start small if you must—every monumental success begins with a single, small step.

And yes, the path of an entrepreneur is strewn with challenges. It's not the absence of obstacles but your reaction to them that defines your business journey. Persistence, savvy decision-making, and learning from each stumble are your keys to navigating these hurdles.

I encourage you to keep the conversation going. Share your successes and the lessons learned from the hurdles you've faced. Join online forums, connect on social media—keep building a community where support and shared learning pave the way for all of us.

Reflecting on my own path of starting and growing businesses, from the bustling streets of south Louisiana to the dynamic business landscape of Texas, the journey has been nothing short of a rollercoaster. There were many challenges, but every challenge was a stepping stone to greater heights. The fulfillment of pursuing my passion and making a difference through each enterprise has been immensely rewarding.

So, as you turn the last page of this book, don't see it as the end. It's the beginning of your unique story. Embrace your entrepreneurial journey with optimism and determination. Go out there, make your mark, and remember, in the world of business, the sky's just the beginning!

Here's to your success—may your business thrive and your journey inspire!

References

- *Choose a business structure* https://www.sba.gov/business-guide/launch-your-business/choose-business-structure
- *Register your business | U.S. Small Business Administration* https://www.sba.gov/business-guide/launch-your-business/register-your-business
- *Self-Employment: Starting Your Own Business as Felon-ReeCareer.* https://reecareer.com/self-employment-starting-your-own-business-as-felon/
- *Starting a Business: License and Permit Checklist* https://www.findlaw.com/smallbusiness/starting-a-business/starting-a-business-license-and-permit-checklist.html
- *Beginners Guide to Business Insurance* https://bethanyins.com/beginners-guide-to-business-insurance/
- *How to Create an Investor Pitch Deck* https://www.svb.com/startup-insights/startup-strategy/how-to-create-investor-pitch-deck-vc-angels/
- *Top 10 Crowdfunding Campaigns of 2023 So Far* https://go.indiegogo.com/blog/2023/08/top-10-crowdfunding-campaigns-of-2023-so-far.html
- *SBA Loans vs. Conventional Bank Loans: How to Choose* https://www.nerdwallet.com/article/small-business/sba-loan-vs-bank-loan
- *Bootstrapping: How to Bootstrap Your Startup* https://carta.com/learn/startups/fundraising/bootstrapping/
- *21 Effective Low-Cost Marketing Strategies to Kick-Start ...* https://ppcexpo.com/blog/low-cost-marketing-strategies-for-startups
- *The Ultimate Guide to Create a Brand Identity [FREE TOOLKIT]* https://www.columnfivemedia.com/how-to-create-a-brand-identity/
- *SEO for Small Businesses: Everything You Need to Know* https://www.investopedia.com/seo-for-small-businesses-8584627
- *The Benefits of Networking for Business Growth and Success* https://www.linkedin.com/pulse/benefits-networking-business-growth-success-ebube-julius
- *11 Proven Examples of Sales Funnels that Convert* https://www.freshworks.com/sales/sales-funnel-examples/
- *The 7 Best CRM Software for Small Businesses in 2023* https://salesdashcrm.com/top-crm-small-business-2023/
- *How to Overcome Sales Objections and Win More Deals* https://www.close.com/blog/sales-objections

- *21 Loyalty Program Examples — and Why They Work So Well* https://loyaltylion.com/blog/customer-loyalty-program-examples
- *Best Startup Tools to Try in 2023 [150+ Tools and Resources]* https://www.upsilonit.com/best-startup-tools
- *Kanban vs. scrum: which agile are you? - Atlassian* https://www.atlassian.com/agile/kanban/kanban-vs-scrum
- *How to implement just-in-time (JIT) inventory management* https://business.adobe.com/blog/basics/how-to-implementing-jit-inventory-management
- *13 essential cybersecurity tips for small and medium enterprises* https://nulab.com/learn/software-development/cybersecurity-small-medium-enterprises/
- *The complete guide to startup risk assessment - FasterCapital* https://fastercapital.com/content/The-complete-guide-to-startup-risk-assessment.html
- *35 Legal Mistakes Every Startup and Growing Business Must ...* https://www.crowdspring.com/blog/legal-mistakes/
- *Best Practices: Contract Drafting and Collaboration* https://www.contractworks.com/blog/best-practices-contract-drafting-and-collaboration
- *Recruiting strategies: a comprehensive guide for small ...* https://resources.workable.com/tutorial/recruiting-strategies-a-guide-for-small-business
- *Employee Onboarding Best Practices: The Ultimate Guide* https://hronboard.me/blog/employee-onboarding-best-practices/
- *15 Essential Leadership Skills Every Entrepreneur Should Cultivate* https://www.forbes.com/sites/forbescoachescouncil/2023/01/11/15-essential-leadership-skills-every-entrepreneur-should-cultivate/
- *Startup Culture: What It Is, Why It Matters and How to Build It* https://builtin.com/company-culture/startup-culture
- *7 Successful Business Pivot Examples - WDHB* https://wdhb.com/blog/7-business-model-pivots-you-can-learn-from-d721cbfbea36/
- *Emerging markets conclude 2023 on better note than ...* https://www.spglobal.com/marketintelligence/en/mi/research-analysis/emerging-markets-conclude-2023-on-better-note-than-developed-markets-jan24.html
- *How a small company used big data to increase its sales* https://www.imd.org/research-knowledge/marketing/articles/how-a-small-company-used-big-data-to-increase-its-sales/
- *International Market Entry Strategies For Businesses* https://www.forbes.com/sites/forbesbusinesscouncil/2023/10/19/international-market-entry-strategies-for-businesses/

Risk Assessment Worksheet

Asset or Operation at Risk	Hazard	Scenario	Opportunity for Prevention or Mitigation	Probability (L, M, H)	Impacts with Existing Mitigation (L, M, H)					Overall Hazard Rating
					People	Property	Operations	Environment	Entity	
1	2	3	4	5	6	7	8	9	10	11

Instructions

Column 1: Compile a list of assets (people, facilities, machinery, equipment, raw materials, finished goods, information technology, etc.) in the left column.

Column 2: For each asset, list hazards (review the "Risk Assessment" page from Ready Business) that could cause an impact. Since multiple hazards could impact each asset, you will probably need more than one row for each asset. You can group assets together as necessary to reduce the total number of rows, but use a separate row to assess those assets that are highly valued or critical.

Column 3: For each hazard consider both high probability/low impact scenarios and low probability/high impact scenarios.

Column 4: As you assess potential impacts, identify any vulnerabilities or weaknesses in the asset that would make it susceptible to loss. These vulnerabilities are opportunities for hazard prevention or risk mitigation. Record opportunities for prevention and mitigation in column 4.

Column 5: Estimate the probability that the scenarios will occur on a scale of "L" for low, "M" for medium and "H" for high.

Columns 6-10: Analyze the potential impact of the hazard scenario in columns 6 - 10. Rate impacts "L" for low, "M" for medium and "H" for high.

Column 8: Information from the business impact analysis should be used to rate the impact on "Operations."

Column 10: The "entity" column is used to estimate potential financial, regulatory, contractual, and brand/image/reputation impacts.

Column 11: The "Overall Hazard Rating" is a two-letter combination of the rating for "probability of occurrence" (column 5) and the highest rating in columns 6 – 10 (impacts on people, property, operations, environment, and entity).

Carefully review scenarios with potential impacts rated as "moderate" or "high." Consider whether action can be taken to prevent the scenario or to reduce the potential impacts.

From ready.gov/business